How to be Happier and Wiser

How to be Happier and Wiser

Seven Easy Steps to Relaxed Wisdom

by

Geoff Pridham

WisdomBooks

Lulu Books
www.lulu.com

Copyright © 2006 by Geoffrey Robert Pridham

First Published 2008

ISBN 978-1-4092-7890-0

All rights reserved. No part of this publication may be reproduced, stored in a retrieval system, or transmitted, in any form or by any means, electronic, mechanical, photocopying, recording or otherwise, without the prior permission of the publisher.

This book is sold subject to the condition that it shall not, by way of trade or otherwise, be lent, re-sold, hired out or otherwise circulated without the publisher's prior consent in any form of binding or cover other than that in which it is published and without similar condition including this condition being imposed on the subsequent purchaser.

Illustrations by Geoff Pridham

Contents

The Possum and the Wombat

The possum was having a normal day. He was working hard on his farm. He had to take care of himself and make sure his family was provided for. He had little choice but to work and work throughout the day to keep everything running. His wife often said to him that she wished he could earn more so the family would be better off. But she also complained if he was away from home for too long. He was not sure what he should do. Should he work longer to make more money or should he spend more time at home and be happy to live on less? But then what would his wife say? And the kids wanted more things! It was a problem.

Sometimes the possum thought the solution would be to move to a different area. Perhaps this place was all farmed out. Maybe if he moved to a more productive area he would be able to grow more crops and still be able to spend more time with his family. But who was to say that his wife wouldn't continue to complain and his kids wouldn't still ask for more? Perhaps that was just our nature – to always want more and more, to never be satisfied. The possum didn't know.

"A lot to think about," thought the possum, "and in the meantime I have to keep working and working and growing more crops."

A difficult life!

Where was this more productive area anyway? Was it in another country, or a nearby area? Where could it be? Perhaps he needed to change professions. What if he took up a job in the town in an inn, or a shop? Then he could be paid more money and forget about the farm. The kids might appreciate him being able to buy more for them. On the other hand, they might have to move to the town and live side-by-side with other creatures. They might not like the hustle and bustle of town life.

"Yes, a lot to think about," thought the possum, "and no easy way to decide." Perhaps all these thoughts were on the wrong track.

The possum was not happy with his own life either. He had a lot of questions. Was this all there was? Was this as good as it gets? He wondered about the causes of his own dissatisfaction. Maybe he was being unreasonable too, just like his wife and kids. Maybe satisfaction was something that came from within … maybe it was foolish to seek it outside.

The possum mentioned his concerns to a few creatures and one day the echidna said to him: "Why don't you go and see the wombat? She knows a thing or two. She might be able to advise you on what to do with your life ... she is extremely wise and really knows her stuff."

The possum thought this sounded like a good idea and set out to meet the wombat at her home.

* * *

"So what is your problem?" the wombat asked the possum, peering at him shrewdly across the kitchen table.

"My problem, Mrs. Wombat, is that I'm not happy with my life," replied the possum.

"I see," said the wombat.

"Yes, that is why I've come to speak to you," explained the possum.

"Why me?" asked the wombat. "Why did you think I'd be able to help you?"

"Oh! I was talking to Echidna and he said you were extremely wise and really knew your stuff," replied the possum, looking embarrassed.

"That's very kind of Echidna!" said the wombat. "I hope I can live up to his recommendation.

"Well then, Mr. Possum, what exactly is this problem you are having with your life?"

"I don't even know if this makes sense," said the possum. "You see, I work all day raising crops to make money for my wife and kids, but I don't feel satisfied about it. When I get home my wife says: 'Is that all you've made?' and my kids just want more and more. Maybe it's my fault, maybe I should be more productive, or find a more productive area to farm in. Or maybe it's my wife and kids' fault – maybe they should want less out of life … maybe they should be happier with less. I don't know. I don't know who is in the right myself.

"That's part of the problem, Mrs. Wombat, I don't know what makes sense and what is just folly in life. I feel discontented, restless and uncertain. But I still have to go on making a living, what else can I do? I have responsibilities, others depend on me, no matter how I feel," concluded the possum.

"Well!" said the wombat. "You certainly have a problem there. I hope you didn't think I was some kind of counselor or psychiatrist. That's not my field at all."

"No, no. I didn't come to you for that," said the possum. "What I heard was that you are extremely wise. I wondered if you'd be able to give me guidance on that."

"On wisdom?" asked the wombat. "You came to ask me about wisdom?"

"Yes. If you think that would help me to know what is important and what is not important in life … and how to deal better with other creatures," replied the possum.

"Hmm. I think I might be able to help you with those things," said the wombat thoughtfully. "Why don't you give me a try and see what you think?"

"Thank you very much, Mrs. Wombat. I look forward to it," said the possum.

"Okay. Let's begin," said the wombat. "What you need, my dear sir, is a kind of 'relaxed wisdom'. This is what I teach. Nothing frantic, nothing hectic, nothing dramatic or exciting! No, I teach relaxed, calm, happy wisdom. Through this I think you will know what to do, Mr. Possum!"

The possum nodded.

"Good," smiled the wombat. "'Relaxed wisdom' comes from understanding yourself – how your mind works," she explained. "Would you like to hear about that?"

The possum nodded again.

"Good. Who you are, Mr. Possum, is basically three creatures. You have your emotional boss, your trusted adviser and your true self."

"Okay," said the possum.

"Yes, I should explain that I am not speaking precisely, in academic terms, but practically, in terms that will be useful for us," said the wombat. "As long as you are happy with that we can proceed."

"What you need, my dear sir, is a kind of 'relaxed wisdom'."

"Oh, I'm happy with being practical," said the possum. "In any case, I don't have the time to make a life-long study out of this."

"That's fine then," said the wombat. "Leave the life-long study to me and I'll just give you what you need to make things work."

"Excellent!" agreed the possum.

"You are, as I said, basically three creatures – in practical terms. But you don't often realize this. The first creature you are is your emotional self – the one that feels. This feeling self can be quite bossy – telling you what to do – so I say they are like an 'emotional boss' in your life. I often describe them as being like an emotional emu running back and forth in your mind and making a lot of noise.

"The second creature you are is the one you go to for advice based on your experience and what you think about things. This creature is like a 'trusted adviser' whom you can ask for advice or specific information. They don't do much thinking, they base their advice on what they've seen before. I describe them as being like a serious tortoise who sits quietly at a desk surrounded by files about your experiences in life.

"Finally, the third creature you are is the real you, the thinking you, the one who says: 'Wait a minute! What's going on here?'"

"So *that's* the real me," laughed the possum. "Now I know why I came here! Or was it my emotional boss who told me what to do?" he smiled.

"Probably a mixture," answered the wombat seriously.

"My emotional boss was upset so he said: 'Do something! Go and see that wombat or something! Quick!' Then my trusted adviser said: 'Maybe you can go and see that wise wombat you've heard about from Echidna. Maybe she can help.' Then I said: 'Okay!', and here I am!" concluded the possum.

"Yes, here you are," smiled the wombat. "I think you are understanding my little model of the conscious mind well."

"Thank you, Mrs. Wombat," said the possum.

"Okay. Let's think of an example in your own life. Tell me about something that's been bothering you at home."

"Sure. My wife has been saying from time to time that I'm not making enough money, that we are not doing as well as we should," said the possum.

"Right."

"So, to use your model, I'd say that when she is saying this it triggers off some strong feelings in my mind. My 'emotional boss' gets going and he tries to tell me what to do. He says: 'You don't have to take that kind of nonsense, you don't deserve that. You work hard. What does *she* do? Just complains and complains: nag, nag, nag!'"

"Then what do you say?"

“Me? I guess I try to think about that. Maybe I go to my ‘trusted adviser’ who checks what’s in the files of my memory and says that I’m not being reasonable – I mean, my ‘emotional boss’ is not being reasonable. After all, my wife does a lot in the household, and I’m not sure that she isn’t right about how well I should be doing. Perhaps I should be doing better and making us more prosperous.”

“Okay. So then what happens?” asked the wombat.

“Then I try to decide,” said the possum. “Sometimes I think my wife is not so guilty, other times my emotional boss wins and I think she is just nagging. Then I get even angrier and argue with her. Later I feel guilty and try to make up.”

“Okay, fine,” said the wombat. “So, do you see that your anger and guilt are coming from your ‘emotional boss’?”

The possum nodded.

“And most of your thoughts are based on the words of your ‘trusted adviser’, and these are often confusing and unresolved?”

“Yes, I see that,” agreed the possum.

“And finally it is you, your real self, that is running around trying to satisfy the demands of your emotional boss while still following the advice of your trusted adviser – do you see that?”

"Yes, I do. It is my real conscious self that is trying to sort all this out … and not doing all that well, I guess!"

"Yes, not doing all that well," agreed the wombat, "but that is what we're here to correct."

The possum nodded.

"How do you like what I've said so far?" asked the wombat.

The possum considered. "I do like it, Mrs. Wombat," he said after a moment.

"Good. Then I will teach you," said the wombat.

1 Ask an Expert!

"The first relaxed wisdom technique I want to tell you about, Mr. Possum, is to 'Ask an Expert!'," said the wombat.

"Like I'm doing with you," said the possum.

"Precisely," agreed the wombat. "But before I explain this to you I want us to visit a problem in your life and see how you handle it now. Then we can see how different the situation would be if you applied this relaxed wisdom technique.

"Okay," agreed the possum. "What should I choose?"

"Anything you like," answered the wombat. "How about the problem you're having with your wife?"

"Yes, all right," said the possum.

"Let's imagine visiting her now. I'll keep quiet and just watch. You can act as normal."

The possum nodded.

* * *

"Why does life have to be so hard with you?" the possum's wife demanded. "Why can't you make more money? Look at your children. They're dressed in rags!"

"Why does life have to be so hard with you?"

"I don't think they're rags," the possum replied, but then regretted saying it. He didn't mean to argue, but his wife did say such irritating things!

"Well what do you call them? What do you want them to look like? They need new things, they look like they're wearing hand-me-downs!" she said angrily.

"Oh honey, don't exaggerate," said the possum. "It doesn't help anyone."

"Oh really?" said his wife. "And what do you want me to say?"

The possum sighed. What was the point of this discussion if she couldn't be reasonable about it?

"Well?" asked his wife.

"Well, we'll see," said the possum. "Maybe something can be done about our prosperity. I'm not sure. And I don't feel like doing much about it when you keep going on at me like this," he blurted out.

"Yes, well if I didn't you wouldn't do anything," replied his wife, but then looked ashamed that she had said it.

"Oh honey, I'm sorry," said the possum.

"Me too," said his wife, "but it had to be said."

The possum frowned and went silent.

His wife remained silent too.

* * *

"Yes, I see your problem," said the wombat. "Before I tell you about the first relaxed wisdom technique, I'd like to illustrate what this was like inside your mind. Using my little model I'll describe what your emotional boss, your trusted adviser and your true self were doing here. If you remember, your emotional boss is like an emotional emu and your trusted adviser is like a serious tortoise.

* * *

"Why does life have to be so hard with you?" the possum's wife demanded. "Why can't you make more money? Look at your children. They're dressed in rags!"

"What's this?" said the emotional emu. "What's going on here? I don't like this. Do something about it. We're under attack!"

The true self, a possum, nodded. "I'll ask the trusted adviser."

"Well, hurry up!" said the emu. "We haven't got much time. I'm frightened."

"Okay," said the possum. He walked over to the serious tortoise.

The tortoise looked up from his notes. "How can I help you, Possum?"

“I need to know what’s going on with my wife. The emu is upset. What should I do?” asked the possum.

“Hmm. Let me see,” said the tortoise, looking through the files on his desk. “Wife … arguing. Yes, I have it here,” he said, pulling out a file.

“Hurry up!” called the emu frantically.

“Your wife is unreasonable,” the tortoise read from the file. “She is too demanding. You should resist her.” He smiled over his glasses at the possum. “Okay?”

“Thanks, Mr. Tortoise,” said the possum. “Okay, we’ll resist her!” he called to the emu.

“Resist? Okay. I hope that works,” said the emu.

“I don’t think they’re rags,” the possum replied, but then regretted saying it. He didn’t mean to argue, but his wife did say such irritating things!

“I don’t think this is such a good idea,” said the emu. “I’m frightened. We don’t need to argue.”

“Well what do you call them? What do you want them to look like? They need new things, they look like they’re wearing hand-me-downs!” she said angrily.

“I knew this wouldn’t work,” said the emu. “Do something!”

The possum turned to the tortoise.

“Hmm?” said the tortoise. “Some more advice? The file says she is unreasonable and you should resist.”

“Okay,” said the possum.

The emu gulped.

"Oh honey, don't exaggerate," said the possum. "It doesn't help anyone."

"Oh really?" said his wife. "And what do you want me to say?"

The emu hid his head.

The tortoise looked on, smiling.

The possum sighed. What was the point of this discussion if she couldn't be reasonable about it?

"Well?" asked his wife.

The possum was getting the hang of this – resist the unreasonable demanding woman. "Well, we'll see," said the possum. "Maybe something can be done about our prosperity. I'm not sure."

The emu suddenly ran around and around. "I can't take this any more!" he cried.

"And I don't feel like doing much about it when you keep going on at me like this," the possum blurted out.

"Yes, well if I didn't you wouldn't do anything," replied his wife, but then looked ashamed that she had said it.

The emu noticed this and felt ashamed too. He was not an argumentative bird. "What have you done?" he asked the possum.

"Oh honey, I'm sorry," said the possum.

"Me too," said his wife, "but it had to be said."

The emu looked irritated again. "What was that?" he asked.

The tortoise pointed knowingly at the notes in the file.

The possum frowned and went silent.

His wife remained silent too.

* * *

"So that's my version of what was going on inside your head," said the wombat. "What do you think of it?"

"Yes, it's interesting," said the possum. "I certainly didn't realize I had an emu and a tortoise inside my head! But seriously, I think it really helped to explain how the emotional boss and the trusted adviser affect how I make my decisions."

"Thank you," said the wombat. "Let's look at the first relaxed wisdom technique now and see how it works.

"'Ask an Expert!' is like bringing an expert along to talk to your boss and straighten out his demands. If your emotional boss has to answer to an expert before he tells you what to do then he's going to have to make a lot more sense."

"So I'm arguing with my wife at home and I bring an expert into the room?" queried the possum.

"If you like!" laughed the wombat. "No, of course I didn't mean that. But what you could do is see a marriage counselor. If your wife agrees you could both visit an expert like that and get them to help with your problem. I know that's rather drastic, and you probably don't want to go that far at this stage, so you can 'Ask an Expert!' in a different way."

"I certainly didn't realise I had an emu and a tortoise inside my head!"

"Okay."

"Yes, you could read, for example. You could read a book by an expert on dealing with marriage difficulties. Then when you were having an argument with your wife you could remember what the expert wrote and apply that. Effectively you would be using the expert for advice as the argument occurred – as if they were in the room with you," said the wombat.

"That doesn't seem all that dramatic a technique," said the possum.

"No, it isn't," agreed the wombat, "yet it is remarkably effective. You'd be surprised how easily the expert can calm your mind and help you get control of yourself again – even when they are not really there and you are just imagining them."

"Imagining them?"

"Yes. As you did with the expert who wrote the book, you can imagine the expert is with you and see what advice they would give. You can even do this with creatures you've never met but have just seen on television, or in a movie, or only heard about. As long as you can imagine them being in the room with you and your wife they can give you advice and calm you. This way you can be pursuing a kind of 'relaxed wisdom' in no time," said the wombat.

"I see. So let's try that out. I'm going to imagine I am with my wife now and it's not going well and see what happens," proposed the possum.

"Okay. Go ahead," agreed the wombat.

* * *

"Why does life have to be so hard with you?" the possum's wife demanded. "Why can't you make more money? Look at your children. They're dressed in rags!"

"I don't think they're rags," the possum replied, but then regretted saying it. He didn't mean to argue, but his wife did say such irritating things!

"Well what do you call them? What do you want them to look like? They need new things, they look like they're wearing hand-me-downs!" she said angrily.

Now I must remember something, thought the possum. What was it? It was hard to think through the cloud of emotion that was enveloping him. Oh yes, now he remembered. He had to 'Ask an Expert!'.

"What do you want to know?" asked the possum's imaginary expert – the wombat.

This is strange, thought the possum, talking to someone in your head at the same time as you're arguing with your wife!

"Are you listening to me?" his wife demanded.

"Yes honey," the possum answered. But he kept thinking about the imaginary wombat.

"What do you want to know?" the wombat repeated.

"What should I do about my wife?" the possum asked.

"Well, then answer me!" said his wife.

The wombat considered. "You should think about what's really bothering her," advised the wombat. "Later when you've got some time you should go over what it is that she could really be upset about. But for now I suggest that you just try to calm her."

"Sorry honey. I'll think about what you said and see if there's anything I can do," said the possum with some difficulty. His emotional boss was fighting with him – demanding that he take revenge and not demean himself in this way.

"Why try?" said his wife. "I'm not sure you would be able to come up with anything."

The possum looked at his imaginary expert adviser. The wombat looked back and raised an eyebrow.

"Well, I'll see," said the possum calmly. "Then we can discuss this again."

The possum's wife looked at him with a puzzled expression. "This is not like you," she said.

The possum nodded, feeling a little surprised himself.

"I guess your discussions with that wombat are paying off," his wife said.

The imaginary wombat smiled.

"I guess so," said the possum.

* * *

"So what were the emu and the tortoise doing in that situation?" asked the possum.

"The emu was being corrected by the expert in your mind," replied the wombat. "When he tried to speak and tell you what to do the expert was also speaking. You had to listen to one or the other of them and decide whose advice or demands you would follow."

"And what about the tortoise?" asked the possum.

"He had to compete with the advice of the expert as well. He read from his file about your wife being unreasonable but the expert was advising you to be more considerate and try to calm her. Again you had to choose whose advice to follow," said the wombat.

"I see," said the possum. "It's lucky that I listened to the right creature!"

"You see, the way 'Ask an Expert!' works," said the wombat, "is to introduce an alternative 'boss' into the equation. Your emotional boss will be having to deal with this other boss who is giving orders as well. Which one will win? It depends on how much you respect the new boss in your life, how much you value their opinion. If you are thinking of someone who means a lot to you then you will be much more likely to listen to them than to your emotional boss."

"It's like having someone important in the room with you," said the possum.

"Yes, quite like that," agreed the wombat. "Of course, an imaginary expert cannot have as strong an effect as a real one, but they are better than nothing!"

"Yes, it was like that in the example with my wife," said the possum. "It went much better than just trying to rely on myself to control my mind. It was very helpful."

"In a crisis you may not be able to get a real expert to attend, so the imaginary one is especially useful then," added the wombat. "One last point, the expert doesn't have to be someone you would be able to meet, they don't even have to be earthly. For example, you may imagine a spiritual being, if you respect that sort of thing."

"Really! So if I was religious I could imagine my respected spiritual authorities in order to control my emotional boss," said the possum.

"Precisely," confirmed the wombat. "You could do that. It can be very powerful to imagine this if you really believe in a religious view."

"I don't believe in any particular religious view," said the possum, "but I do believe there are a lot of things we don't understand in life, a lot that remain unexplained."

"And is there any particular creature or being you can imagine as an expert who stands for these things?" asked the wombat.

"Hmm. Not really," replied the possum. "I think I'll stick with using you as my main expert."

"Thank you," said the wombat. "I'm flattered."

"Not at all," said the possum. "To me you are very much a 'respected authority', so imagining you helps me to regain control of myself when my feelings are strong."

The wombat smiled happily.

* * *

"You kids try to behave yourselves!" the possum said crossly to his children later that night.

His daughter and son looked around in surprise.

"What's wrong, Dad? We weren't doing anything," objected his daughter.

The possum was fed up. His children had been making a lot of noise all evening and he wanted to rest. It had been a hard day – working on the farm and then studying with the wise wombat.

That made him think. The wise wombat – what would she advise now? The possum imagined the wombat here, in the house with him and the kids. What would the wombat say?

"You're being emotional. You're overreacting," the wombat said.

"Hmm. I think you're right," thought the possum. "But those kids have been making a racket all night."

"Really?" questioned the wombat. "Is that really true? And what was your solution to this problem?"

"To shout at them, I guess," replied the possum, smiling at himself a little.

"And that is relaxed wisdom?" probed the wombat.

"No. Of course not," thought the possum. "It is just my emotional boss telling me what to do. I wonder what I should really do?"

The children were still looking at their father, waiting for him to speak.

"May I give you some advice?" asked the wombat. "You should show the same respect towards your children as you would expect for yourself, and you should not react emotionally to their disturbances. Don't let your emotional boss make your decisions for you."

Good advice, thought the possum. His emotional boss was no longer in control.

"Sorry," the possum said to his daughter. "I'm just a little tired and wanted some peace and quiet."

"That's all right, Dad," said his daughter. "We'll go and play in the other room."

"Thank you," said the possum. "That's very thoughtful."

His wife looked on in astonishment.

* * *

Later that evening the possum was thinking. What if I am on the wrong track with my life? What if my wife is right and I should be doing better? What if I have no idea what I'm doing?

The questions were starting to irritate him. He decided to consult his imaginary expert wombat to help get his feelings under control.

"Listen, I don't want to wait until tomorrow. Can I talk to you now?" the possum asked his imaginary wombat.

"Sure, but you do understand I am *imaginary*, don't you?" teased the wombat.

"Yes, of course I do," the possum replied. "Is that a problem?"

"Only in the sense that anything I say now will be coming from your own head, your own imagination," said the wombat. "What I mean is that I may be able to help you to be calmer and more relaxed in your wisdom, but I can't give you advice about things you don't know or can't imagine."

"I see," said the possum. "That makes sense. So you can't tell me things that the real wombat knows but I've never heard of, but you can help me to think, can't you?"

"Yes, I can help you to think more clearly," replied the wombat.

"Okay. Then let's proceed," said the possum. "My problem is I'm not sure if my life is on the right track. Maybe my wife is correct and I should be doing better."

The wombat considered. "Hmm. And what do you want me to say?"

"Tell me if my life makes sense or if I should be doing something else. Or tell me what a sensible life should look like," suggested the possum.

"A sensible life should look wise," answered the wombat. "It should be wiser and happier with a kind of 'relaxed wisdom'. I don't know much about your life because you haven't told me about it yet, but I do know that you're not happy and you're seeking answers. This is good but it does suggest to me that you have some level of problems."

"You are right," said the possum. "I do have some level of problems. I may not be doing as well as I should be, my wife does not always agree with me, my children don't always respect me, and I'm not sure what I should be doing or what 'wisdom' is."

"And you don't feel happy about that," prompted the wombat.

"No, I don't. And I don't even know if that's reasonable, if that makes sense," said the possum.

"Right."

"So what can you tell me?" asked the possum.

"What I said today: that you need a kind of 'relaxed wisdom' about these things," replied the wombat. "For instance, you can use the technique of consulting experts, even imaginary ones, to help you get control of your emotional boss and think more sensibly about your life."

"But that doesn't tell me what life I should lead," complained the possum.

"My dear sir, it can't do!" retorted the wombat. "But you could study the experts on what a 'successful' life is, or the ones that talk about forming better relationships with other creatures, and add to your knowledge through that."

"But that would take some effort and it's difficult to determine which experts to trust," objected the possum.

"Sorry about that!" laughed the wombat. "It's far too much to ask of someone that they do some work in order to get on better with creatures and know what is the better thing to do!"

"All right, all right," muttered the possum. "You've made your point, and it's a valid one, but I am tired and I think I will sleep now."

"As you wish," said the imaginary wombat. "I'll see you tomorrow … in real life."

Things You Can Do

Here are some "Ask an Expert!" activities you could do now, or you could skip to the next chapter and come back to these later if you like.

1. Think of some situations in your life that are not going as well as you'd like. What experts could you ask for advice? What do you think they might say?

2. Is there any situation you face today where consulting an imaginary expert in your head might help you to be calmer? Who would you choose as your imaginary expert? Is it someone you know or someone you've heard of or is it a spiritual being … or something else? How much do you respect this person, (because the more you respect them the better this will work)?

3. Think about the emotional boss in your head: are they like an emotional emu? If you had to choose an animal to describe them which one would you pick? Do you think there could be a better way to describe them? Are they always the same or are they like different things at different times?

4. Think about the trusted adviser "tortoise" in your head: how much do you think they know? How accurate is their information and the conclusions they've drawn? What do you think is in their files about your life? How much do you trust what they're telling you?

5. This is the tough one! How can you know which expert to trust? How do you choose the right one when they don't all agree with each other? What do you think is the answer to this?

2 Go Inside!

“A second relaxed wisdom technique we can devise from the nature of our mind is to ‘Go Inside!’,” said the wombat. “This is based on moving our viewpoint from its usual position on the outside of a problem to the inside of it.”

The possum nodded.

“Let’s choose a situation in your life and imagine it without relaxed wisdom,” said the wombat.

“Okay,” agreed the possum.

* * *

“You don’t always keep your room clean,” the possum said to his son. “Why is that?”

The possum's son looked at his father for a moment, wondering what this was all about. "I'm not sure, Dad," he said cautiously.

"Well, what are you going to do about it?" demanded the possum.

"Keep it clean, Dad," answered his son.

"You said that before," complained the possum. "Make sure you do it this time, or there'll be trouble."

"Yes, Dad," said the possum's son.

* * *

"That's great," said the wombat. "A good example. Now let's imagine what was going on inside your head."

* * *

"Why doesn't my son keep his room clean?" complained the emu. "I've told him enough times. Do something about it, Possum!"

"Okay, okay. Don't get upset. I'll ask our trusted adviser," said the possum. He went over to the tortoise. "What should we do about my son?" asked the possum.

The tortoise looked up from his desk. "I'll check," he replied, and pulled out the file on the possum's son.

"It says here," continued the tortoise, "that he is a young man and that he should show respect."

"I see," said the possum. "So he should respect me as I am his elder and his father."

"That makes sense," agreed the tortoise, looking through his file notes. "It matches the file."

"Okay. I know what to do, thank you," said the possum.

"You don't always keep your room clean."

"You don't always keep your room clean," the possum said to his son. "Why is that?"

The possum's son looked at his father for a moment, wondering what this was all about. "I'm not sure, Dad," he said cautiously.

Yes, not showing respect, thought the possum to himself. I'll straighten him out. "Well, what are you going to do about it?" he demanded.

"Keep it clean, Dad," answered his son.

I'd better make sure he really means it, thought the possum. "You said that before," he said to his son. "Make sure you do it this time, or there'll be trouble."

"Yes, Dad," said the possum's son.

* * *

"Okay. Happy with that?" the wombat asked.

The possum nodded.

"Then, to continue, the second relaxed wisdom technique is to 'Go Inside!' the problem. We can go inside the mind of the other creature, or inside the nature of the other thing, or inside the overall situation," said the wombat. "As I said before, we are similar to other thinking creatures, having an emotional boss and a trusted adviser, and we can use these similarities to help us understand others. For example, if you were talking to your wife and you wanted to understand what was going through her head you could ask yourself what her emotional boss and trusted adviser might be saying."

"That sounds good," said the possum.

"Yes. It is helpful for understanding, and it is also helpful for controlling your emotional boss," said the wombat.

"How so?"

"Well, when you are thinking 'inside the mind' of the other creature it is difficult to be as emotional about them as you would be if you were thinking 'inside your own head', as it were. For a moment it is as if you really were the other creature, and you start to see things through their eyes. They may have been irritating you, but now you will see how you might have been irritating them! Whatever is motivating them and they are remembering will be in your mind. You won't be thinking about your own feelings and ideas about the situation."

"But you can't know exactly what they are thinking and feeling," objected the possum.

"No, of course not," said the wombat, "but you can have a pretty shrewd idea."

"How?"

"'How' is to ask yourself about your own experiences. Your feelings are similar enough to other thinking creatures for you to understand them. For example, what did you think your wife was feeling when she was arguing with you?"

"Anger, frustration, exasperation," said the possum.

"And have you ever felt those things?"

"Sure. Of course."

"So if you cast your mind back to when you felt those things then you will be remembering similar feelings to your wife," said the wombat.

"But it's not fair that she should think like that," objected the possum.

"That may be, but she's feeling that way no matter what you say," pointed out the wombat. "And it's useful to you, helpful, to find out what she is feeling and experience that."

"Why?"

"Because, as I said, it will help you gain control of your emotional boss and be able to be more rational in your mind," replied the wombat. "And it may also help you to deal with the other creature better," she added.

"I see," said the possum.

"Now, the other thing you can do is remember ideas from your past where you felt or acted in a similar way to your wife."

"But I didn't!" said the possum.

"Of course you did," contradicted the wombat. "You just have to think about it to remember an occasion. For example, have you ever been frustrated with someone … or something?"

"Well, yes. I have," admitted the possum.

"There you have it," said the wombat. "If you have ever had a similar experience where you have been frustrated by someone or something then you can remember what thoughts you were having at the time. These will give you an idea about what thoughts your wife is experiencing."

"Really? How?"

"Let's give it a try," said the wombat. "Think of the time when you felt frustrated with your son for not keeping his room tidy."

"Okay."

"Now what was it about?"

"I remember I asked my son to tidy his room and when I went to check it was still messy," said the possum.

"So do you remember what you were thinking and feeling at the time?"

"Yes. I remember I was particularly annoyed that he hadn't listened to me and I felt frustrated that I had to keep repeating myself. 'Why should I have to do that?'

I thought. 'He should just listen to me and do what I say.'"

"So you're getting an idea of what you were thinking and feeling at the time," said the wombat. "Now consider what your wife might be thinking and feeling based on that."

"Based on my own experience? Well, I guess she could be thinking that she is sick of having to repeat herself to me. I should 'clean up my act' and make more money for the family and do what she says."

"Okay. And how might she be feeling?"

"Frustrated that she has to keep repeating herself, and annoyed that I haven't listened to her," suggested the possum.

"That sounds possible, doesn't it?" said the wombat. "So you're getting an insight into how your wife might be seeing the situation."

"Yes, I am," agreed the possum. "And I suppose it's reasonably accurate, as you say."

"I think so. Accurate enough, anyway," said the wombat. "So what do you think? Has this helped you to be calmer and more reasonable when you're in these situations?"

"Possibly, possibly," said the possum. "But I wonder if she is really in the right or not."

"As, no doubt, might your son," said the wombat.

"My son? But he's just a child," said the possum.

"Still, if you were to think from his point of view you might see the possibility that he doesn't agree with you."

"Hmm," said the possum. "Hmm. Maybe you're right."

"If you think about how you feel when your wife is criticizing you then you might get some insight into your son's state of mind."

"Yes, I do," agreed the possum. "Interesting. Again, I'm not sure that he is right but I do get some insight into his state of mind!"

"That's good. That's all you need at this stage in our discussion," said the wombat.

* * *

"You don't always keep your room clean," the possum said to his son later that night. "Why is that?"

The possum's son looked at his father for a moment, wondering what this was all about. "I'm not sure, Dad," he said cautiously.

The possum thought for a moment. What might his son be thinking and feeling? When had a similar thing happened to him? He cast his mind back to when his father had questioned him about his behavior. Yes, he remembered scenes like that. And what had he been thinking and feeling at the time?

The possum remembered that he had felt tense and a little resentful. Why had his father been asking that? What had he done wrong now? Deep down he had even wondered what right his father had to ask him these questions – he wasn't perfect either, was he?

Okay, thought the possum, let's try to put these insights into practice for dealing with my son.

"What I mean," said the possum, "is that none of us here is perfect but we do try to work together to look after this place."

"Yes, Dad," said his son.

"So I know that it's not always easy to keep the house clean."

"Yes, sometimes we're too busy or it doesn't really matter because no one is coming around," agreed his son.

"Precisely," said the possum. "But what I was asking was why you don't always keep your room clean … but I see that you have answered that. We may be too busy or it doesn't really matter."

"Yes, Dad," said his son. "But if you think that's a problem I'll do better."

"That's all right," said the possum, guessing that his son still felt tense. "I'll discuss it again if I think there's something you should know."

"Okay, Dad," said his son.

* * *

"Let's see what the emu and the tortoise were doing when you 'went inside' the problem," said the wombat during their discussion the next day.

* * *

"Why doesn't my son keep his room clean?" complained the emu. "I've told him enough times. Do something about it, Possum!"

"Okay, okay. Don't get upset. I'll ask our trusted adviser," said the possum. He went over to the tortoise. "What should we do about my son?" asked the possum.

The tortoise looked up from his desk. "I'll check," he replied, and pulled out the file on the possum's son. "It says here," continued the tortoise, "that he is a young man and that he should show respect."

"I see," said the possum. "So he should respect me as I am his elder and his father."

"That makes sense," agreed the tortoise, looking through his file notes. "It matches the file."

"Okay. I know what to do, thank you," said the possum.

"You don't always keep your room clean," the possum said to his son. "Why is that?"

The possum's son looked at his father for a moment, wondering what this was all about. "I'm not sure, Dad," he said cautiously.

The possum thought for a moment. What might his son be thinking and feeling? When had a similar thing happened to him? He cast his mind back to when his father had questioned him about his behavior. Yes, he remembered scenes like that. And what had he been thinking and feeling at the time?

The possum remembered that he had felt tense and a little resentful. Why had his father been asking that? What had he done wrong now? Deep down he had even wondered what right his father had to ask him these questions – he wasn't perfect either, was he?

Okay, thought the possum, let's try to put these insights into practice for dealing with my son.

"But he's not showing respect!" complained the emu. "What are you going to do about that? We can't have that."

"Now, now," said the possum. "My son is probably feeling tense and a little resentful – let's deal with that."

"That's not the advice in the file notes," said the tortoise. "It says here that he is a young man and should show respect."

"That's because I did not 'Go Inside!' my son's mind before," replied the possum. "If this works please update the file notes."

The tortoise nodded.

The emu waited, looking tense.

"What I mean," said the possum, "is that none of us here is perfect but we do try to work together to look after this place."

"Yes, Dad," said his son.

"So I know that it's not always easy to keep the house clean."

"Yes, sometimes we're too busy or it doesn't really matter because no one is coming around," agreed his son.

"Precisely," said the possum. "But what I was asking was why you don't always keep your room clean … but I see that you have answered that. We may be too busy or it doesn't really matter."

"Yes, Dad," said his son. "But if you think that's a problem I'll do better."

"That's all right," said the possum, guessing that his son still felt tense. "I'll discuss it again if I think there's something you should know."

"Okay, Dad," said his son.

The emu relaxed.

The tortoise smiled and made a note in the file.

* * *

"Mr. Possum," began the wombat, "'Go Inside!' is useful for understanding what is going through the mind of another creature, but it can also be used to understand groups of creatures or even situations themselves."

"That is interesting, Mrs. Wombat. How is it done?" asked the possum.

"Well, what do you think, Mr. Possum? How would you try to 'Go Inside!' the minds of a large group of creatures?"

"That's not easy," said the possum. "I'm not sure. You couldn't imagine every creature's mind in a large group, so I suppose you would have to do something else. What could it be?" He paused to think. "I guess you'd have to use some trick, like imagining only a few of the creatures."

"That's right, Mr. Possum," said the wombat. "If you imagine just a few representative creatures, or even just one, then you can 'Go Inside!' their minds and see what they are thinking and feeling. This will give you some insight into what the group is thinking and feeling."

"A useful trick," said the possum, "but how accurate is it likely to be?"

"A lot more accurate than trying to imagine the inner nature of these creatures through some other means," replied the wombat. "No, of course it's not magic, but it is a sensible way of trying to go inside the mind of a group. As long as you remain aware that what you are doing is very general then you can draw general conclusions."

* * *

The possum tried to imagine the general nature of the mind of female creatures who had trouble with their husbands. He wasn't female, so he would have trouble imagining this accurately, but he thought he'd give it a try.

"When did I have trouble with my 'husband' – in a general sense?" thought the possum. He guessed it was like general trouble with wives. What was that like? Like what he experienced with his own wife – only, more general. The possum could imagine that – the frustration, the annoyance, the thoughts: "Why can't they be more like us? Why do they have to be so different? Why can't they understand us and think like us?"

Yes, these were thoughts he could understand. So, in general, in his region, female creatures with troublesome husbands could be thinking thoughts like these, and feeling frustrated, irritated and annoyed. It made sense.

* * *

"Apart from 'going inside' the mind of a group of creatures, we can also go inside a situation, or even inside the nature of an unintelligent creature or mindless device," said the wombat.

"How is that possible?" asked the possum. "Especially when none of these things has a mind like us?"

"Of course it's not the same as imagining the mind of another intelligent creature, but it is useful for gaining control of yourself and can even give you an insight into the situation. For example, if you wanted to go inside the situation with your wife you could ask yourself what its 'inner nature' may be and see what that tells you," said the wombat.

"Okay, so it's not my wife's mind I am thinking about but the inner nature of the situation itself," said the possum. "I guess that makes me think about biology and the general nature of marriage relationships. I suppose it's the inner nature of marriage to seek a better life together and one partner or the other might be pushing for that at some time."

"Yes, that is possible," agreed the wombat.

"But what is a 'better life' really?" asked the possum. "I suppose one partner might be wondering about that while the other is pushing for more wealth."

"It could happen," said the wombat. "Or the first partner may just be being lazy or feeling frightened of change."

"Yes. That is possible," agreed the possum, frowning.

"Anyway, that was just an example of 'going inside' the nature of a situation rather than the mind of some creature," said the wombat.

"I see," said the possum. "Thanks for explaining it."

* * *

Later that night the possum sat in his house and wondered what was "inside" the situation of living a more prosperous life. His current location only allowed him to grow a certain amount of crops – if he moved somewhere else would he be better off? Or was this just greed? Was greed good in these cases?

He tried to think what the inside of this might be. Could it be that we thinking creatures had a desire for a better life – that this was natural? Maybe not everyone felt like this, but a lot of creatures did. So was this the inside of the situation: a kind of average thinking creature which had a desire for more in its life? That sounded about right.

The possum thought back to when he had desired more in his life. He rarely desired more material possessions for himself, but he would have liked to have been able to give them to his wife and children. He remembered how he felt that kind of gnawing in his heart and that feeling of intense frustration in his mind when he wished he could provide more for his family, but the world was not helping him. Life on the farm, if anything, was getting tougher. He had to work harder and harder to grow the crops. What a terrible feeling it was to think about such things! It made him feel inadequate and hopeless, someone deserving of the world's contempt.

"So my wife must feel like that," thought the possum, "something like that. And the general situation of living a more prosperous life has an inside that is about frustration, feeling inadequate and hopeless, and desiring more for yourself and your family. Interesting."

But he could not see how this made him more relaxed about it. Still, it did make him a little wiser about what was going on. That could lead to "relaxed wisdom" about the situation over time.

"Yes," thought the possum, "if my desire for more is just my emotional boss trying to tell me what to do then I should be able to find ways of bringing him under my control. Especially with the help of Mrs. Wombat." He smiled quietly to himself.

Things You Can Do

1. Think of some situations in your life where other people are involved. Ask yourself when you had a similar experience to them. It doesn't have to be exactly the same, just similar enough. What were you thinking and feeling at the time? Go over your memory of that for a while. Try to relate that to what the other people might be thinking and feeling – could it be something similar to what is in your own memory?

2. Take a situation with other people involved and using your memory of similar events in your own life try to come up with better ways to deal with those people. How would you like to be treated in that situation? Can you think of better ways to treat other people based on this?

3. Consider a situation where you were upset by someone's behavior: if you had "gone inside" their mind would it have made you a little less upset with them, (even if you don't agree with what they did)?

4. Try out the method for understanding groups of people by imagining a few or even one representative person. What kind of conclusions can you draw from "going inside" their minds? How accurate do you think this is? Is it useful for understanding other groups of people in a general way? What groups do you think people would put you in?

5. Try to imagine the "inner nature" of some situation that's been bothering you – does this give you any useful insight or make you feel any calmer about the problem?

6. The tough one: how accurate do you think your understanding of other people really is? Even when you "Go Inside!" their minds, how different do you think your memories of your feelings and ideas are to theirs? Given that your feelings and ideas are different, how much are they the same?

3 Get Away!

"Let's pick another situation in your life, Mr. Possum," suggested the wombat.

"Okay," said the possum. "I have been concerned about how well I've been doing in life."

"Think about that then, but try to add the emotional boss emu and the trusted adviser tortoise to it," instructed the wombat.

"Okay, Mrs. Wombat," said the possum.

* * *

The possum thought about the significance of how well he was doing in his life. What should he have achieved and how should he have achieved it?

"Yes, how? And what?" said the emotional emu. "It's so disturbing. Creatures will laugh at us, they will say we are failures," he warned.

"Possibly, possibly," said the possum.
"But how do we know they are right or should be listened to?"

"I don't know," said the emu, "but it still disturbs me. It's not pleasant to have creatures laugh at you or look down on you."

"No," agreed the possum. "I'll ask the tortoise what he thinks."

The possum walked over to the tortoise, who was sitting at his desk.

"Mr. Tortoise, what do you advise about what we should have achieved in our lives and how we should have achieved it?" asked the possum.

The tortoise looked down at his desk and searched through the files. He muttered to himself as he searched. "Yes, I think this file would apply, Mr. Possum," he said eventually. "It is called 'Being Seen by Others'."

The possum nodded.

The tortoise looked at the file notes. "The notes say that being seen by others can be embarrassing and stressful and most unpleasant. Yes, that's about it," said the tortoise.

"Gosh. I don't like the sound of that," said the emu. "Let's not get into the public eye then!"

"I'm still confused," said the possum. "I don't know how to succeed or what success means. I think maybe I should just keep quiet and let things stay the way they are until I get a better idea."

"Sounds good to me!" said the emu.

The tortoise closed the file and put it back on the desk.

* * *

"Okay, that's very good, Mr. Possum," said the wombat. "Let's look at the third relaxed wisdom technique: 'Get Away!'"

The possum nodded.

"Yes, if you can get away from the situation, creature or thing then the problem will be over."

"But you can't always get away," complained the possum, "or it may not be the most desirable thing to do. For example, I can't really get away from my wife and kids, and I may not really want to."

"But they still cause you aggravation," said the wombat. "Even a little time away from them may help to reduce the pressure, and you can also use another

'Get Away!' technique, which is to get away from them within your own mind."

"Within my own mind? That sounds strange," said the possum.

"Not so strange really," said the wombat. "Thinking creatures do it all the time, especially when they gain perspective on the situation."

"Yes, that makes sense," said the possum. "So if I can gain perspective in my own mind then it's equivalent to my getting away from the situation."

"Yes it is," confirmed the wombat. "Of course it's not as good as really getting away from the situation, but it's the next best thing."

"I see."

"Now what this does for you, apart from making you feel better, is to allow you to see things as they really are. If you are upset by a situation you have a natural tendency to forget its real importance in your life. You tend to see it as vital, as essential – you feel that 'something needs to be done and done now!' … and that's not always true. If you can gain perspective then you may be able to judge what's essential and what is not," said the wombat.

"That sounds helpful," said the possum. "How is it done?"

"By any technique you like where you imagine something that gives you perspective," replied the wombat. "For example, you could imagine looking back at your life from your grave: 'What was important? What didn't really matter? What was worth spending your time on? What wasn't?' That sort of thing. And with this 'view from the grave' you should be able to judge whether the current situation is essential or not. If it's not important why worry about it? Why let your emotional boss tell you what to do?"

"Good point," said the possum. "Why should he tell me what's important in my life when *I* should be deciding?"

"Yes indeed," said the wombat.

* * *

The possum thought about how well he was doing in his life. What should he have achieved and how should he have achieved it, especially if he looked at it from the grave?

"The grave?" said the emu. "What do you mean by that?"

"You know, like Mrs. Wombat said, it is looking with the perspective that we all die, so we can see what's really important to us in our lives," answered the possum.

"Oh, I see," said the emu. "I thought you were being morbid, but that's rather a nice idea."

"Yes, isn't it?" agreed the possum.

The emu looked calm and relaxed. "So what is important to us?" he asked dreamily.

"I'll ask the tortoise," said the possum.

The tortoise looked through his files. "I think it's in here," he said, pulling out a folder: "'The Things That Really Matter'."

"What does it say?" asked the possum.

The tortoise looked at the notes. "Family, friends, happy moments, saving creatures' lives, living your dream, sunsets, staying true to your principles …," he read.

"Hmm. That's nice," said the emu, sitting down.

"Yes, those are important things," agreed the possum.

"The list goes on," said the tortoise. "Actually, it's rather long."

"Never mind," said the possum, "I get the idea. I'll start by looking at family. What will I leave for them when I am in my grave? A memory? Or money? What is more important for them?"

He imagined asking his son what he would want left for him after his father was gone: a memory of good times spent together or a bit of money and a memory of a father who was never there? What would his son say? The possum wasn't so sure what his son would say, but he was sure about what he'd *want* him to say: a memory of a father who was there for him.

How well was the possum doing in his life? As well as the creatures who mattered to him felt about his presence in their lives. That's what "Get Away!" told him.

The emu smiled happily.

The tortoise had gone back to studying his files.

* * *

"Thinking of the grave is not the only way you can get perspective on your life," the wombat advised. "In fact, if you don't like that method then you should come up with one you do like. It is better to use a method you enjoy because you are more likely to repeat it."

"Yes, I think it could be a bit morbid to look from the grave," said the possum.

"Very well," said the wombat, "then let's devise another way to 'Get Away!' from the situation. What would you prefer?"

"I don't know," replied the possum. "Maybe I could imagine the view from another place or time. But what place or time? Does it have to be real, or will anything do?"

"Anything that takes your fancy," said the wombat. "As long as you enjoy it."

"Okay. Then I would like to look from the point of view of climbing high in the trees," said the possum.

"If that gives you perspective then that's the thing for you," said the wombat.

* * *

The possum imagined the view from high in the trees. He had climbed to the highest place he could and was looking over the treetops to the distant lands below. The scene looked beautiful and tranquil from up here. What would he say now about the situation with his wife and kids?

It didn't seem all that important any more. It was a problem, yes, but in the scheme of things it was not such a big one. Maybe he had been overreacting to the situation, maybe he could take things a little easier. From high in the trees he felt much better about his life.

"Yes, I'm not so badly off," smiled the possum.

The view from high in the trees.

* * *

"What method do you use to 'Get Away!' in your mind, Mrs. Wombat?" asked the possum.

"Me? I use the method of burrowing as deep as I possibly can. I imagine that I have burrowed to the deepest possible burrow in history and I look at the situation from there. Things can seem a lot less troubling if you can look at them from so deep a place."

"Yes, that is interesting," said the possum, "though I'm not sure I could imagine it. Still, it would work for some creatures!

"What else could you do, Mrs. Wombat? Do you know any other methods?"

"Yes, of course. There are a myriad – as many as you can make up. One I have heard of is to 'Think Like a Rock'. In this method you imagine your mind is like a rock and the troubles of life are like water just running over the surface. They can't really bother you because they can't get inside. Your timeless 'rock-mind' will outlast them."

"That's a very somber method, Mrs. Wombat," observed the possum.

"Yes, I suppose it is, but some creatures find it comforting."

"I think I'll stick with my treetops!" said the possum.

"As you wish," said the wombat. "And I'll stick with my deep burrows."

* * *

"There's one last thing I'd like to emphasize," said the wombat, "and that is the possibility of getting away from situations physically. You should bear in mind that the ultimate calming ‘Get Away!’ method is to actually get away physically, not just escape within your own mind. I know this sounds obvious but it is often forgotten. Even if you can’t get away for all time you may be able to take ‘time out’ and just go for a walk around the block. This can help clear your mind so you can think more rationally about the situation.”

“Yes, a bit of ‘time out’ can often help,” agreed the possum. “It can relax you and give you some perspective on the situation.”

“I see that you understand this. The trick is to remember to do it when you are all fired up about something. If you can do that and tear yourself away from the situation then you will be well on your way to perspective.”

“Yes, a good point. I must remember that,” said the possum.

* * *

“Are you getting anywhere with your talks to the wombat?” the possum’s wife asked that night.

“I think so,” the possum replied.

“What did you learn today? Something useful?” his wife asked.

"I learnt about perspective – how to 'Get Away!'," the possum said.

"So do you want to get away now?" asked his wife irritably.

"Perhaps. Maybe," said the possum, getting annoyed.

"Then why don't you?" his wife demanded.

Why does she get so cross, the possum wondered? But he was feeling pretty fed up himself. He decided to get out of the house and go for a little walk.

"I'll see you later, dear," the possum said, getting up and leaving the room.

The possum's wife watched him leave with amazement. The wombat was really having an effect on him. She wondered how long it would last.

The air was crisp and cool and helped the possum to clear his mind as he walked. A lovely night, he thought. Lovely to be away from his irritated wife and get a breath of fresh air. He felt himself relaxing almost immediately.

As the possum walked he was able to think. Why was his wife so irritated with him? Surely she should be happy that he was learning about relaxed wisdom from Mrs. Wombat. But he supposed she didn't hold out much hope and thought he would still be the same annoying creature in time. Oh well. He'd have to see if he'd be able to change or not.

Later the possum returned to the house and greeted his wife cheerfully. He decided it was better to stay away from the topic of what he was learning from the wombat. Maybe he'd be able to discuss these things on a different day.

Things You Can Do

1. Think of some situations, people or things that you would like to get away from in your life – is there any way you could really get away from them? Why aren't you doing it? Maybe you don't think it is reasonable or necessary to get away from some situations, people or things – how much effort are you willing to make, how far do you want to go?

2. What method would you like to use to "get away" from situations in your own mind? Which method would you enjoy for gaining perspective? Think about some of the known techniques for gaining perspective: looking from the grave, climbing high in the trees, burrowing to the deepest burrow in history, thinking "like a rock", with the troubles of life washing over you like water. Do you like any of these? What other techniques could you come up with? Which is your favorite?

3. Consider some situations you can't get away from or don't want to get away from: is there any way you can take a little "time out" from these in your day? Try adding some time out to your day and see how you feel.

4. The tough one: how are you going to remember to get away from situations that are really troubling you? What method are you going to use to make sure you follow your technique for gaining perspective when you are all fired up and passionate about something?

4 Get Familiar!

“So far we’ve been talking about techniques you can do quickly,” said the wombat. “But there are also relaxed wisdom techniques that you can do in your quiet times to gain long-term advantages.”

The possum nodded.

“Yes. You may not reap immediate rewards, but if you stick with these you should see yourself changing over time to become a much more relaxed and wiser creature,” said the wombat.

“Mmm. I’m willing to make the effort,” said the possum.

“Good. Good,” said the wombat. “Then let’s proceed. This technique is to spend some of your quiet times – like when you are walking along, or ploughing the fields, or just sitting at home – to 'Get Familiar!' with the exact nature of your feelings."

"And why do you do that?" asked the possum.

"The idea is that when you 'Get Familiar!' with your emotions then when your emotional boss comes around telling you what to do you will say: 'Oh, I know that feeling, I'm familiar with that', and he won't be able to push you around as easily. You'll be on to him," explained the wombat.

"So you learn about your emotional boss," said the possum.

"That's right," confirmed the wombat. "Now, the way you go about it is to ask yourself these questions, over and over: 'What exactly was I feeling at the time? What else was I feeling? What exactly?' By asking these questions over and over you will become extremely familiar with your feelings."

"Okay, that sounds good," said the possum. "I'd like to give it a try."

"Go ahead," invited the wombat.

* * *

"Let me see … I remember arguing with my wife," said the possum. "What exactly was I, or my emotional boss, feeling at the time?" He paused to think. "Yes, my emotional boss 'emu' was feeling upset … upset and angry. He wanted me to get revenge, to stand up for myself, to do something about the situation. What else was he feeling? Anger … irritation … depression. Yes, depression! He was wondering if there would ever be an answer, if we were to spend the rest of our lives arguing with my wife. Was this what it was all about? Was there no way out of this situation? The tortoise had reminded us that 'Till death us do part' was the saying when we were married, but now the emu felt like it meant death every day," remembered the possum.

"What else was he feeling? Let's see … he was feeling afraid in some way. What was that about? Oh, I see, he was feeling weak and a bit stupid. Maybe my wife was right about us, maybe she was the stronger partner … maybe she was the wiser and her accusations were well deserved by us. The emu didn't feel sure. He became irritated. After all, wasn't it the responsibility of the wiser creature to assist the weaker one – not just to go ahead and attack them? My wife should be assisting us, not just attacking, if she really was wiser.

"That's interesting," observed the possum. "I didn't realize the emu was feeling like that. Those feelings were hidden among the other ones."

"That's the advantage of using this technique," interrupted the wombat. "You can find even the hidden feelings that your emotional boss was having."

The possum nodded. "I wonder what else he was feeling," he said. "I can't think of anything."

"Then try to be exact," suggested the wombat.

"Okay. Exact feelings. He felt anger, irritation, depression and fear … and I guess he had a sense of injustice as well. Yes, it felt unfair that our supposedly superior wife was attacking us. The emu had a feeling of moral outrage about that. Especially after all the things we'd done for her and the family."

"Anything else?" asked the wombat.

"I'm not sure, but I think I could increase my knowledge of these feelings if I kept getting familiar with them over time," said the possum.

"Yes. And the more familiar the less power they will have to control you."

* * *

What did the possum feel about the incidents with his children? He sat and pondered this later that night. What were his exact feelings? Were there any more – any he hadn't identified before?

"What exactly was I feeling at the time?" the possum asked himself. "At what time?" He tried to recall.

Well, there was the incident of the messy rooms. What exactly had he been feeling about that? He was annoyed, certainly, irritated by his children's carelessness. What else? He had felt depression – the thought that his children may never be "responsible" bothered him. Why couldn't they be thoughtful and considerate like him?

What else had he been feeling? Violence – he had some violent feelings. He guessed he had suppressed these, but deep down he had felt like attacking his ungrateful children and "beating some sense into them". Lucky he hadn't acted on that!

Anything else? He cast his mind back to those times. Despair. He had also felt despair. Maybe all his actions and setting an example in life would come to nothing. His children would go their own way no matter what he did. Maybe his actions were not as good as he thought, maybe he wasn't such a good example. It could all be his own fault that his children ignored him and left their rooms messy.

"Hmm. That's a surprising feeling," thought the possum. "I didn't realize I felt guilty about that."

Was there anything else he was feeling at the time? Tired – he felt tired of having to raise the same point over and over. Why should he have to do that? He should only have to make his point the one time and that should be enough. His children should listen to him and do what he said.

"Amazing," thought the possum. "An amazing set of feelings over one little thing."

Was there anything else he was feeling? Maybe foolish? It may be that deep in his mind the possum also felt foolish about his complaints. He wasn't sure about that, but it could be that a feeling of foolishness was lurking in the back of his mind.

"Well, I think I've done enough for now," thought the possum. "Might as well leave it at that for tonight."

He went to bed.

* * *

"You know, I'm starting to get familiar with my feelings already," said the possum.

"That's good," said the wombat. "It will certainly help you to become wiser, in a relaxed way."

"That will be nice," said the possum. "So the next time I'm feeling angry or depressed I should be able to be more relaxed about it."

"Yes, you should. Your emotional boss will find it harder and harder to push you around because your trusted adviser will be able to remind you about the significance of these emotional responses. He will tell you just how repetitive and misleading they are."

"Misleading, yes, and repetitive, yes. I see that," said the possum.

"I'm starting to get familiar with my feelings already."

Relaxed Wisdom Technique 4:
"Get Familiar!"

Things You Can Do

1. Spend some time getting familiar with your emotional boss. What exactly are they like? What exactly do they feel? How many feelings do you think they have: a few, many, hundreds, thousands? What can you discover? Do you think there are any hidden feelings in your mind? Can you find them?

2. How many of your feelings do you think you should follow? Is it a good or bad idea to obey your feelings? Maybe it is a mixture of good and bad – what do you think? What feelings do you think you'd like to follow without worrying about them? Which ones could you really do without?

3. The tough one: do you think feelings are really separate from yourself or are they part of your being? How could you tell which is which? How do you know who is the real you and who is "outside" and trying to boss you around?

5 Know Yourself!

"There is another technique of relaxed wisdom that works in a similar way to getting familiar with your feelings and that is to 'Know Yourself!'," said the wombat.

"Know what about yourself?" asked the possum.

"Well, you already know more about your feelings, so what other area do you think you need to learn more about?"

"Your trusted adviser, I suppose," replied the possum, "so I guess that means your memory."

"Right first time!" commended the wombat. "You're very smart."

"Why, thank you," said the possum. "I hope I can keep it up!"

"Okay. So now please choose a topic you have some memories about so we can try out the technique."

"I'll pick my wife again," said the possum.

* * *

The possum imagined going to his trusted adviser tortoise about the topic of his wife. What would the tortoise say?

"Your wife is unreasonable and too demanding and you should resist her," advised the tortoise, reading from his file notes.

I remember that, thought the possum. He always says that when she is arguing with me or asking me for something.

"Thank you, Mr. Tortoise," said the possum. "I guess I've got my answer."

The tortoise smiled happily over his glasses and put the file away.

* * *

"Okay, good choice," said the wombat. "So, how do you think you would go about learning more about your memory?"

"I'm really being put to the test now!" said the possum. "I suppose I would do it in a similar way to how I learnt more about my feelings and use a quiet time to get more precise about what I know."

"That's right, Mr. Possum. You need to ask yourself this question: 'What exact memory is that thought based on?' Then you ask yourself what the thoughts in that memory are based on – what *exact* memory, and so on until you arrive at the memories where you can say there's nothing more, those are the original memories for those ideas," said the wombat.

"'The original memories'? What does that mean?" asked the possum.

"What I mean, Mr. Possum, is those memories that are far back or are really important in your life. You will often find that you have not thought those through, yet they are being used to form your basic view about life," explained the wombat.

"So when I go to my trusted adviser he is giving me advice based on unchecked memories?"

"That's right. Not completely unchecked, of course, because they are based on what really happened to you, but given more weight than they deserve. Let me explain.

"Try to imagine what is was like for your trusted adviser when he didn't know much about some topic.

When you came to him with something new to store in the memory he eagerly grabbed it and tried to work out what it meant so he could file it correctly. Then the next experience you brought him had to be categorized and filed. Your trusted adviser would naturally try to file it in the existing categories, if he could find a match. Only when something didn't seem to fit would he create a new category in the files."

"So it's the filing system of my trusted adviser that is causing the problem," said the possum.

"That's right. In practical terms that is what is going wrong – or might be going wrong. You need to check that filing system and make sure that the categories are right," confirmed the wombat.

* * *

The possum imagined going through the tortoise's filing system that related to his wife. What was in the files about her? How had his trusted adviser worked out the file notes that he always read out? How had he categorized and filed the information?

The possum started to apply the technique the wombat had taught him: asking his adviser what exact memory his file notes and classifications were based on.

The tortoise read further into the files, muttering to himself. After a few seconds he said: "Yes. I see an example here, Mr. Possum. You had an argument with your wife where she complained that you weren't attentive enough to your children. She said you didn't show enough interest in them or spend enough time with them. You replied that you were very busy earning money and were tired at the end of the day. You said: 'What do you want? Do you want me to spend my time with the family or for us to be more prosperous? You have to make up your mind. You can't have both.'"

"So," thought the possum, taking a deep breath to calm himself, "what was I thinking at the time? What exact memories was that based on, Mr. Tortoise?"

The tortoise looked through the file. "Possibly you were thinking about the injustice, the unfairness of her view. You were working hard and she was still complaining. You couldn't do everything but she seemed to want it. This sort of thing had happened before, so I classified it as a habit of hers," said the tortoise. "Ever since she had that first big argument with you all those years ago I have advised you that your wife is unreasonable in cases like these."

"What argument?" asked the possum.

"Oh, you remember," said the tortoise. "It was in the early years of your marriage when she said you didn't pay enough attention to her when you came home from work. You said you were tired and you still loved her, and then she got really angry and started shouting at you saying it didn't show."

"Yes. I see an example here, Mr. Possum."

"Oh yes," said the possum.

"Yes. So I classified her behavior as 'demanding and unreasonable' and put that in the file notes," said the tortoise.

"So ever since then you have read those notes and advised me she was being unreasonable," said the possum.

"In cases like this, yes," said the tortoise.

"But it may have only been the first argument where she was being unreasonable and demanding," observed the possum.

The tortoise shrugged and closed the file.

* * *

"How far back do you need to go when you are looking for the exact memory your ideas came from?" asked the possum. "I mean, in the case of my wife I only needed to go back to the first time she had a big argument with me."

"Well, that can be right," said the wombat, "that can be enough. If that gives you insight into your trusted adviser's classifications then you have got your answer. On the other hand, you might learn something more by examining your memories even further. It's up to you. You do what you want."

"What should I ask if I want to go further back on my wife's arguments, since I've already arrived at the first one we had?" the possum asked seriously.

"Well, you could ask yourself what exact memories give you the ideas you have about creatures when they argue with you," suggested the wombat.

"I see. That makes sense," said the possum. "Maybe I tend to automatically classify creatures as unreasonable when they argue with me. It's possible. I guess I could go back through my memories to find which exact ones that idea comes from." He pondered. "You know, I think it was in my childhood when I first figured that out. I remember my school teacher arguing with me in the class about the names of the villages in our district. I was convinced that I was right but she insisted on correcting me. It made me very angry, but there was nothing I could do. When I told my mother about it that night she said that I must be a very difficult student. No one would listen to me. I went and looked up my atlas and saw that I had been right, but it was no use telling anyone. I'd only get into trouble," said the possum sadly.

"Most unpleasant," said the wombat.

"Yes. I remember another major incident at school. I had dropped a subject as I did not have time to study everything I had enrolled for, and the principal had agreed, but when I was attending my last lesson the teacher called me up in front of the class and reprimanded me. He said I was ungrateful and lazy. I said that I was doing weekend studies and the principal had agreed, but this only made him angrier. He said I was insolent and undeserving of his assistance. When I returned to my seat my best friend at the school said to me: 'You deserved it.' I'll never forget that," said the possum.

"A very unpleasant experience," observed the wombat. "So what did you learn from these things – how did your trusted adviser classify them?"

"I think he thought these were examples of the frightful injustice that authorities and friends can visit on us," said the possum.

"So now you have an insight into how he classified your wife's behavior," suggested the wombat.

"Yes. But that doesn't mean she is in the right," objected the possum.

"Of course not. But it makes you understand how you look at the situation," said the wombat.

"It certainly does!" agreed the possum. "Is my wife being reasonable or unreasonable? My trusted adviser will assume the latter. Do I agree with him in this case? I'd have to think about that. Maybe her comments are just another example of the frightful injustice that exists in this world, or maybe they aren't."

"That's right. That's what you need to consider when you get to 'Know Yourself!' better," agreed the wombat.

* * *

As the possum walked home that evening he thought about what his trusted adviser was telling him about his level of success in his life. What classifications was the adviser using for this? What exact memories had he based this on?

The possum thought back. When had "success" first entered into his memories? He thought it might have been at school. He remembered standing in front of the class and being embarrassed by the teacher. He hadn't remembered something the teacher had told them. What was it? He couldn't remember what it was now – something about grammar, he thought. But he did remember how he felt, the terrible shame, the laughter of his fellow pupils, the sarcastic tone of the teacher. He blushed now while remembering it. He had wished the ground would open up and let him disappear into the earth, far from everyone's sight.

So what had the trusted adviser figured out from that? That not remembering important things in public was embarrassing? Something like that. What about other "failures"? Lack of money? Lack of social status? Having the wrong look? Talking the wrong way? Yes, these were all embarrassing things, shameful things. So success, for him, was based on not being embarrassed, on not feeling ashamed of his situation.

"That's rather negative," thought the possum. He supposed it must be the same for a lot of creatures.

What about the positive side of success? What exactly did he remember about that? He remembered that school had not always been about failure. Sometimes he had done well. He remembered when he had got an award for his writing skills. The teacher had asked him to stand in front of the class and handed him a certificate and shook his hand. It had felt good to get the award, but he also wondered what the class was really thinking and if they might start laughing at him again, as they had on the day when he had been reprimanded for his grammar.

"I suppose Mrs. Wombat would say that my trusted adviser had filed 'standing in front of the class' as a potentially embarrassing situation," thought the possum, "so even when I was standing there to receive an award it felt like things could go wrong. I was still uncomfortable when I should have been enjoying it."

That was interesting, what the trusted adviser had said about success. The possum wondered if this suspicion about awards had kept him away from the limelight. Maybe he was a "failure", as his wife had said, because he preferred to keep quietly in the background rather than face that risk of the shame and embarrassment that success could bring. Well, at least, could *seem* to bring – according to his trusted adviser.

* * *

"You know, you might be right about my lack of success," the possum said to his wife when he got home.

"What?" his wife asked, surprised.

"I've been thinking. Maybe I avoid success because I'm afraid of the limelight," the possum explained. "I had some bad experiences when I was young and they seem to have scarred me."

"Really? That's interesting. I didn't know about that," said his wife.

"I guess I haven't really explained everything," said the possum. "I'm just finding out about some of this myself!"

"This is coming from your talks with Mrs. Wombat?" his wife asked.

"Yes, it is," replied the possum. "She has been teaching me about how our memories can determine a lot of what we do."

"Hmm, I see," said his wife. "Well if it makes a change for the better I'll be happy."

"Time will tell," said the possum calmly.

Things You Can Do

1. Spend some time getting to know your thoughts and the memories they are based on. Ask yourself what exact memories your thoughts are based on and keep working back through your memories until you can say there's nothing more. What insights does this give you into why you think what you do? Do you still believe those ideas? How much weight would you give them now?

2. How beneficial do you think it will be for you to know why you think what you do? How much time are you willing to put into this? How will you feel after you have these insights into your own mind?

3. The tough one: think about how much you are yourself and how much you are a product of your own memories. How accurate are your memories anyway? Do you think you remember events where you were highly emotional accurately or less accurately? What does this tell you about who you've become based on your memories?

6 Think Again!

"Today, I'd like to talk about ways to improve how you think," said the wombat. "You need to 'Think Again!' and improve on what you know."

"Sounds good, Mrs. Wombat," said the possum.

"The first way you can improve on what you think is to fix up the records that your trusted adviser is referring to. There are a few ways you can do this. We have already discussed going over your memories to improve on the classifications that your trusted adviser has made from them."

"Yes," said the possum. "That was most helpful."

"Good," said the wombat. "Well, apart from doing this, can you think of any other ways we could improve the records of our trusted adviser?"

"Let me see. I suppose the obvious one would work: to improve the information available by learning more," answered the possum.

"All right. Before we go on, let's pick a different situation to look at in your life," said the wombat.

"Okay," said the possum. "I'd like to return to the topic of whether material prosperity makes sense as a goal in life."

The wombat nodded.

* * *

The possum went up to his emotional emu. "Does material prosperity make sense to you as a way of living a good life?" he asked him.

The emu considered. "It sounds good. It would be nice to have lots of wonderful things. Yes, I'd enjoy that," said the emu.

"Okay, thanks, Mr. Emu," said the possum. He walked over to the tortoise.

"Can I help you?" asked the tortoise, looking up from his desk.

"Yes please, Mr. Tortoise. Does material prosperity make sense to you as a goal in life?"

The tortoise considered. "Hmm." He started to search through his files. "One thing I've said before is that being in the public eye is undesirable and dangerous," said the tortoise as he looked through the files.

"Yes, I remember that," said the possum.

"Yes, there is risk in standing up in front of creatures, as this folder on success shows," said the tortoise, pulling out one of the files. "The notes say that creatures may laugh at you or ridicule you when you're successful. It is better to avoid these exposed situations."

"I see. Thank you, Mr. Tortoise."

The tortoise nodded in acknowledgement and put the file away.

* * *

"I think the information held by my trusted adviser could really be improved in some cases!" said the possum.

"Okay," agreed the wombat. "Can you tell me more about that – for example, what kind of information should you learn?"

"What kind? Oh yes – good quality information, I think."

"And what is that?" asked the wombat.

"Good quality? I guess it means information you can rely on."

"And what is that?"

"The information from experts, I suppose," said the possum. "Not just the opinions of everyday creatures."

"Ah, but are the experts always right, and are the opinions of everyday creatures always wrong?" challenged the wombat.

"Gosh! I don't know," gulped the possum. "I suppose the opinions of experts are not always right, and the information from everyday creatures is not always wrong."

"I should say not," agreed the wombat. "For example, general information from everyday creatures is sufficient to use in a court of law."

"But the court of law also uses the judgment of qualified experts to reach a verdict," said the possum.

"Precisely," said the wombat. "The court accepts the statements of everyday creatures as witnesses to events, and the assessments of experts as opinions worth listening to."

"So what you are saying is 'horses for courses'," said the possum. "We should listen to everyday creatures and qualified experts according to what they really know. That makes sense. But what if the experts are not actually right and the witnesses have got their memories mixed up?"

"That does happen," agreed the wombat, "so you have to be on your guard. But my main point is that you can listen to all kinds of creatures, not just the experts, as long as you bear in mind the level of what they know."

"I see. That makes sense," said the possum.

* * *

"Mrs. Wombat, you're something of an expert on wisdom," said the possum.

"Why, thank you," said the wombat.

"What I mean is that your opinion on what was wise would make sense," explained the possum.

"I hope so," replied the wombat.

"Yes, I'm sure it would," continued the possum. "So if I asked you whether it was wise to pursue material prosperity and worldly success or to be satisfied with what you have then you would be able to give an expert answer."

"I would try," said the wombat.

"Then I could review what is in my memory and correct that," said the possum.

"Okay."

"So what is more important, in your expert opinion, Mrs. Wombat: to pursue material prosperity and worldly success or to be satisfied with what you have?" asked the possum.

"Mr. Possum, what is more important is wisdom. As long as this comes first then you are on the right track. You can indulge your other desires after you have been wise."

"I see. So that says to me that thoughts about worldly success or being satisfied with what you have are coming from your desires, not from wisdom. Your emotional boss is telling you what to do. But you should take control first and determine what should really be happening in your own mind.

"On that basis I will adjust the records of my trusted adviser so that wisdom and desires become the main classification. For example, where he decided that standing up in front of creatures could be dangerous and embarrassing, even if it was to be awarded for success, I should ask him to change that assessment. He should instead say whether if it was wise of my teacher and the class to laugh at me when I got my grammar wrong. Maybe all you could say is that they were causing me to have an emotional reaction. And he should answer the question of why he made a connection between me getting an award and getting a reprimand. The only reasonable connection he could have made was that it happened in public," said the possum.

"That sounds right," agreed the wombat. "Though it's not unusual for creatures to be afraid of standing up in public."

"Then, in terms of wisdom, my wife's desires for material prosperity for our family should not be determining what we will do," concluded the possum.

"Unless they are wise," said the wombat.

"Yes, unless they are wise," agreed the possum.

* * *

"You know, honey," the possum said to his wife that night, "you might be right about our lack of material prosperity. It could just be that I've been avoiding it because of my fear."

"I see," said his wife. "And what are you going to do now?"

"I'm going to think about it," said the possum.

His wife sighed.

"No, seriously," said the possum. "I'm going to think about it and try to decide if it is wise for us to pursue material prosperity or not. And if I decide it is wise I'm going to pursue it."

"Can I have a say in this decision?" asked his wife.

"Of course, honey, of course. All of us can – you and the children," answered the possum.

"Okay then," said his wife. "Tell me when you're ready to discuss it."

The possum nodded.

* * *

"Today let's talk about the second way you can 'Think Again!' and improve on what you think," said the wombat.

"Okay," said the possum.

"We saw that you could go over the records of your trusted adviser and correct them based on the advice of experts and the experiences of everyday creatures. The second thing you can do is to improve the records by being creative in your own head."

The possum nodded.

"Creativity comes in many forms," said the wombat, "but what I will talk about is a simple method of asking yourself new questions – questions you would not normally ask."

"Such as what?" asked the possum.

"Anything, anything at all," replied the wombat. "As long as it's something you would not normally ask. For example, you could ask yourself why you think your wife is being unreasonable when it might be you who is being unreasonable with her."

"I think I asked that already," said the possum.

"Very well. It was just an example. Instead, you could simply ask yourself why you believe she is being unreasonable then," said the wombat.

"Yes, I hadn't asked just that," admitted the possum. "I think I was getting there but I didn't really believe I could be that wrong about her."

"So it's a question you wouldn't normally ask," said the wombat, "and consequently it's worth asking yourself."

"Why is that? I mean, what use is asking questions like this?"

"These new questions are like going to your trusted adviser and challenging his interpretations," said the wombat. "It's like you jump over his desk and pull out his files and rearrange them to see what other classifications they may bring. For example, you could rearrange his files on worldly success to see what else they could mean."

"So I'm being creative by rearranging my memories," said the possum.

"That's right," confirmed the wombat. "Apart from rearranging the files there's something else you can do when asking new questions: you can add something extra to the files and see how they look with that. For example, when looking at your memories about worldly success you could add the idea that ‘No one in the whole world is reasonable’, least of all yourself, and see what new ideas this brings to your mind.”

“‘No one in the whole world is reasonable’ – so my memories of worldly success are about me and others being unreasonable. It makes some sort of sense,” said the possum.

“Good. Good. Well that’s just one example. The important thing is to try out different combinations and new ways of looking at things and not just be complacent about what you already know,” said the wombat. “Shake up your trusted adviser and give him a hard time and have fun in the process,” recommended the wombat.

“Yes, I will,” agreed the possum.

* * *

“Mr. Tortoise, in regard to your file on success and being in the public eye, I put it to you that ‘No one in the whole world is reasonable’,” said the possum.

“Yes?” said the tortoise, looking up in surprise.

“Yes,” said the possum. “I mean, take a look in that file. What does it say about the time when I stood up in front of the class and got my award and everyone smiled at me?”

The tortoise scanned the file, looking puzzled. "It says that happened in your early school days. The teacher and your classmates congratulated you and gave you an award for your writing skills."

"Yes, but what if they were all being unreasonable?" said the possum. "Have you considered that?"

"Well, no," replied the tortoise. "Is this based on a former experience or some other file's notes?" he asked.

"You're having an experience now," said the possum. "Please take notes."

"Okay," said the tortoise, picking up his pen.

"Our teacher and classmates may have been unreasonable to give us an award and congratulate us," continued the possum, "as 'No one in the whole world is reasonable'."

The tortoise wrote some comments into the file and looked up.

"Perhaps our writing skills were something we shouldn't have been awarded for. Maybe the award should have been for emotional independence," suggested the possum. "I never saw anyone get an award for that at school, but maybe that's what reasonable creatures would have given awards for – not for mere writing skills."

The tortoise made some more notes.

"On the other hand," the possum continued, "what about the time we were reprimanded for our errors in grammar? Would reasonable creatures do that? I suppose it would depend on whether it was really our fault or not. Perhaps it was our teacher's fault that we could not learn easily. Or perhaps it was more reasonable for the teacher to encourage us rather than haul us up in front of the whole class and abuse us," said the possum. "Or perhaps it was unreasonable of us to be upset by the teacher's abuse and the class's laughter. Maybe we should have looked on them with sadness – it was a sign of their own deficiency and probable unhappy future."

The tortoise finished adding notes into the file. He turned to the front page and added to his file notes summary: "The public may be unreasonable in what it punishes or awards us for."

* * *

"Mrs. Wombat, what exactly is the use of asking all these new questions in your mind?" asked the possum.

"It improves the quality of what is in your memory and the advice given by your trusted adviser," replied the wombat.

"Yes, I know," said the possum, "but what use is that really? I mean, how useful is it compared to all the effort you have to make?"

"Oh, very useful, Mr. Possum," said the wombat. "Over time you will reap generous rewards from using your quiet time in this way. When you face a new situation or find yourself in a crisis you will be well prepared for what is going to happen – much better prepared than someone who doesn't spend some of their quiet time improving the quality of the information that is in their memory. Your improved knowledge and the greater flexibility in your thinking will assist you tremendously in life."

"I see," said the possum. "That is interesting – I'll certainly practice this technique in my quiet times."

"Good," said the wombat. "And don't forget to enjoy it when you're doing it too."

* * *

"Maybe you are completely reasonable in expecting me to provide a better life for our family," the possum said to his wife that night.

"I think so," said his wife.

"I thought you might say that!" laughed the possum.

His wife looked mystified.

"Yes, well why not?" asked the possum.

His wife didn't know what to say. Her husband was acting strangely. She felt uncomfortable.

"It's okay," said the possum. "I'll take a look into the matter and see what can be done. No reason to fret," he smiled.

"All right," mumbled his wife. "That sounds good."

Things You Can Do

1. Think about what kind of information you can rely on: is it from experts or everyday people or your own mind? Are there experts whom you can trust? Which ones would you like to learn from? What about everyday people – what could you learn from them about real life situations? Which people do you believe? In your own mind – which information is reliable and which do you need to think about again?

2. Try asking yourself new questions about the things you've always believed. Do they bring up any new ideas? Spend some time trying this out – it's a creative exercise that may give you some surprising new insights if you try it for long enough.

3. The tough one: do you believe that some of your ideas don't require investigation? Which ones? Are you willing to check them anyway or ask yourself new questions about them, or do you think it's a waste of time? Where should you draw the line between what's worth checking and questioning and what you should just leave alone?

7 Make Perfect Decisions and Add Happiness!

"The last thing I want to talk about, Mr. Possum, is how to 'Make Perfect Decisions and Add Happiness!'" said the wombat.

The possum nodded. "That sounds helpful," he said.

"Oh yes, it is," said the wombat. "Imagine being able to do that – to make a perfect decision and still be happy about it. And also to be able to add more happiness to your day. Would you want to be able to do that?"

"Yes, I would," said the possum.

"As usual, please choose a situation in your own life that we can use as an example – one where you have to make a decision and be happy about it," said the wombat.

"Okay. I know what I'm having trouble deciding," said the possum.

* * *

"How much material wealth and worldly success should I pursue for my family?" asked the possum.

"I think they could do with a lot," replied the emotional emu. "We could all use a lot more wealth and worldly success – life would be so much nicer."

"What do you think, Mr. Tortoise?" asked the possum.

The tortoise looked up from his desk. He was not as confident these days, after his recent encounters with the possum. He wondered what the possum might challenge about his file notes today. "I'll check the files," he said, and started searching through them. After a while he sighed and picked up the folder on success in the public eye.

"All I can say," said the tortoise, "is that being in the public eye can be upsetting, but that may be because other creatures can be unreasonable in their judgments. This may mean you should avoid being seen by other creatures, or it may mean you shouldn't care about it. I'm not sure."

"Thank you, Mr. Tortoise and Mr. Emu," said the possum. "I see there is a conflict between our desires and our memories. Also, there are some things we really need to think about – I guess we've been avoiding these issues for some time."

The tortoise and the emu nodded, looking a little puzzled.

* * *

"Very well. Perfect decisions then: what are these? What I mean by this is that your emotional boss doesn't interfere in your decisions and tell you what to do in the first phase of your thinking. Your decisions are first made rationally and wisely," said the wombat.

"Right," said the possum.

"But I am not saying that they have to be boring or unhappy ones," said the wombat. "After you have looked at the decision rationally in the first phase of your thinking you can then consider its emotional aspects and choose the option that suits you best. Your emotional boss gets a 'second chance', as it were."

"Lucky him!" said the possum. "But how does he get that chance if in the first phase of our thinking we have been entirely rational and eliminated all of the interesting and happy options?"

"Ah, good question," said the wombat. "I'm glad you asked. Simply, we don't have to eliminate all of the interesting options, or the happy ones, in the first phase of our thinking."

"I see," said the possum.

"Yes. Rationality allows us to leave some of these in, because we don't have to be completely rational in our lives," said the wombat.

The possum looked puzzled.

"No, we only need to be *rational enough*," explained the wombat. "We can be as happy as we like – there's no limit needed to that – but in terms of rationality we only need enough to get through our lives."

"And how much is that?" asked the possum.

"A little more than many creatures think," said the wombat. "But not that much. You just need to consider what will give you a reasonably healthy and reasonably long life. Many creatures seem to ignore the future in order to get something today, but that is just their emotional boss telling them what to do," explained the wombat.

"So we need to control our emotional boss and consider the future as well as today," said the possum.

"That's right," confirmed the wombat. "We need to be rational enough in our decisions to get by."

"We need to be rational enough in our decisions to get by."

* * *

"So how much material wealth and worldly success does my family need to be rational enough and get by?" asked the possum later.

"What do you think?" asked the wombat.

"Hmm. Well I suppose they need good health, sufficient food and shelter, and no trouble with the authorities," suggested the possum.

"That sounds reasonable," agreed the wombat.

"So they need very little, in fact," said the possum.

"That's true," said the wombat.

"Then the rest is just extras – things done for happiness, or social esteem, or for the convenience of the emotional boss."

"Of course."

"And that's okay, is it?" asked the possum.

"It can be," replied the wombat. "Provided your primary requirements are rational you can add extras for the sake of happiness. The difference between you and other creatures is that you do this deliberately, or 'on purpose'."

"And that's important because I am in control?" questioned the possum.

"It can save you a lot of trouble and unnecessary hardship," replied the wombat, "because you are only doing what's really necessary for survival and to be happy over the long haul – both today and into the future."

* * *

"Honey, we don't need to be all that rich to be happy," the possum said to his wife that night.

"Is this from your talks with that wombat?" his wife asked.

"Yes," the possum replied. "She said that it is important to be rational in the first phase of our thinking and to set minimum levels for what we need at that point. We are allowed to be emotional in the second phase and select the things that make us happier at that stage."

"Let me see if I understand this," said his wife. "In the first phase of your thinking you have decided that we don't need to be rich?"

"Yes. We just need the minimum for survival and companionship," said the possum.

"And when did you decide that we didn't need to be rich to be happy?" his wife asked.

"Ah! In the second phase – because we can be happy with lesser things, and the trouble it takes to get more would not be worth it," said the possum.

"So you say," said his wife, "but I don't necessarily agree with you. For example, do you think we have enough things now?"

"Now? Maybe not," said the possum. "After all, we're not happy now, are we? No, I think we could afford to have more things."

"So you do agree with me," said his wife. "I suppose you thought I wanted a lot, but I really just wanted a little more for us and the children."

"I see," said the possum. "Well, that makes sense."

"I'm glad you agree," said his wife.

The possum smiled quietly.

* * *

"My wife wants us to be richer, Mrs. Wombat, but only enough to be happier," said the possum.

"That sounds promising," said the wombat. "But how much is enough?"

"We haven't discussed that yet, but I think she is coming around to a more reasonable view," replied the possum.

"Good. I'm glad to hear it," said the wombat. "Just make sure you set a maximum effort you are willing to expend to get more wealth. You might also consider how much wealth you will need before you can really be happy – after all, it shouldn't take that much."

"I agree. These are good points and I'll make sure I raise them with my wife," said the possum.

"Yes. You can be happy in other ways than by just living with the results of your decisions," said the wombat. “For instance, you can add more happy experiences to your day – quite deliberately. Why not build up your happiness additionally?”

“So you do things that make you happy just for the sake of happiness?” asked the possum.

“That’s right. And why not?”

“Why not indeed!” laughed the possum. “I suppose the only thing to watch out for is when they interfere with your plans, or when they are bad things – the things you shouldn’t really do.”

“That’s true,” agreed the wombat. “You can add happy experiences to your day, but they should not be things that you ought not to do, obviously. You should choose things that are rational enough to pass the first phase of your thinking but which are also very satisfying to your emotional boss. Happy emotional things, but things that are also wise.

“It’s a question of balance,” said the wombat. “You have to balance the rationality and the happiness in your life.”

“A little bit of each and not too much of either?” suggested the possum.

“No, I’d say enough rationality but not so much it destroys your happiness, and as much happiness as you can rationally get away with," corrected the wombat.

"Yes, of course," agreed the possum.

* * *

"Hello honey," the possum said to his wife and kissed her cheek.

"What was that for?" his wife asked.

"Just adding some happiness to our day, beautiful," the possum replied.

"Another of the wombat's ideas?" asked his wife.

"Yes."

"I'm starting to like this wombat," his wife smiled.

"Me too," said the possum.

* * *

"Let's look at making these 'perfect decisions' some more, Mr. Possum," said the wombat.

The possum nodded.

"Say you want to be richer so you can be happier. 'How much richer?' is what you've got to ask yourself. How much wealth do you need to be happier? And how much can you afford to have or expect to have?"

"How much wealth can I afford to have? Meaning how much effort am I willing to put in to getting it?" asked the possum.

"Yes, that's right," confirmed the wombat.

"So I set these levels in consultation with my family: how much do we need to be happier, how much effort are we willing to put in, and how much wealth can we expect to gain? Wouldn't this lead to conflict, Mrs. Wombat? I mean, isn't it likely that we are going to want more wealth than we can expect to make – more than we are willing to put in the effort to gain?"

"Of course that's likely, Mr. Possum," agreed the wombat. "That's the point of saying these things. It brings them out into the open where you can examine them and make rational decisions about them."

"I see," said the possum. "So we can decide in spite of the desires of our emotional boss."

"Precisely, Mr. Possum, that's it precisely."

"Then what's the point of pursuing happiness through wealth? Wouldn't we be better off learning to be happier with less, or what we already have?" asked the possum.

"Maybe, but it's not necessary, Mr. Possum," answered the wombat. "You're allowed to be wealthy if your rational side says it's okay to pursue this. It's not necessary to turn your back on this possibility at this stage in your thinking."

* * *

"Listen, we want more wealth but we also want to spend time together," the possum said to his family later that night.

"Why can't we do both?" asked his son.

"Sometimes we can," agreed the possum, "and sometimes we can't. Then we have to choose: how much wealth and how much time together? We can't always do both."

"Right, Dad, that's okay. Then let's get a bit more wealth and spend a bit more time together," said the possum's son.

"Okay," said the possum. "What do the rest of you think?"

"I think that would be nice," said his daughter.

"A little more wealth might not be enough," said the possum's wife, "but it would be nice to spend more time together."

"Then let's do that," said the possum. "I just have to work out how, but at least I know what we're aiming for."

"Half the battle," agreed his wife and smiled at her husband.

Things You Can Do

1. Think of some decisions you have to make in your life. Do you tend to be too rational or too emotional in your approach? Try to decide by being just "rational enough" in the first phase of your thinking, and then as emotional as you like in the second phase. What did you choose? How does that compare with what you'd normally choose?

2. What things make you happy? Are they all things that are good and that you ought to do? Try to select some that are not too harmful and okay to do. Can you do any of these today? Try adding them to your day and see if they make you feel better about your life.

3. Think about the things that would make you very happy in your life: how much effort are you willing to make to achieve them, how much sacrifice are they really worth to you? If you were "rational enough" which ones would you choose to pursue?

4. The tough one: what do you think is the correct balance between being sensible and enjoying our lives? Would you rather be more sensible or do you want

to “go for it” and enjoy your time on earth? Which approach gives you the most comfort and happiness?

Other Ways of Being Happier and Wiser

"Mrs. Wombat, I want to thank you for telling me about all these techniques for being happier and wiser," said the possum the next day.

"Not at all, Mr. Possum. It's been a pleasure," said the wombat.

"Before I go I'd like to ask you how your techniques compare with other techniques that creatures use in the world, such as 'Positive Thinking' or 'Rational Skepticism' or other methods."

"Mr. Possum, I didn't invent these relaxed wisdom techniques myself, I learnt them from my teacher and they have been around for some time," said the wombat. "But to answer your question, I believe these wisdom and happiness techniques work a lot better than the other methods you have mentioned. You may be able to combine some of the other techniques with the ones I have taught you, but some are not really useful at all. Let's start by looking at how other techniques might work.

"As with relaxed wisdom, other techniques for being happier and wiser can only work by doing things inside our heads to our emotional boss or our trusted adviser, or by doing things outside our heads that make our emotional boss happier or our trusted adviser seem smarter," explained the wombat.

"Right," said the possum. "If our emotional boss is happier then we are happier, and if our trusted adviser is wiser then we are wiser."

"That's right," said the wombat. "All the other techniques in the world work in these ways. For example, the technique of 'Positive Thinking' works by psyching us up and making our emotional emu happier about doing things that would normally frighten him or sound too hard."

* * *

"I'm not sure that it's worth the effort to try to get wealthier," said the emotional emu.

"Don't be like that," said the possum. "Try to think positively about the situation. We can do this!"

"But I'm not sure I even want to try," said the emu.

"Think about how it will be when we succeed and we are rich," said the possum. "Won't it be wonderful to travel in a luxury car and live in a magnificent home? Think how happy our wife and children will be. No more arguments – our wife will look up to us and admire us for our achievements. Our home will be a happy home."

"Maybe," said the emu, looking interested. "It could be nice."

"Of course it could," said the possum. "Just think about it – how wonderful it will be."

"Hmm," said the emu. "I think you're right. What do we have to do?"

"We just have to pursue our wealth together," replied the possum. "I'll ask our trusted adviser and we'll get started, okay?"

"Okay. Fine with me," said the emu happily.

* * *

"That sounds good, Mrs. Wombat," said the possum. "What's wrong with that?"

"Nothing," said the wombat, "assuming that it is really possible to achieve the goal you are aiming for. But if the goal is not really achievable then you are wasting your time and misleading your emotional boss. Better to be sensible about what you are doing and also be happy than to try to achieve the impossible."

"Yes, that makes sense, Mrs. Wombat," agreed the possum. "But if the goal is really achievable then what is wrong with thinking positively about it?"

"Mr. Possum, you surprise me!" complained the wombat. "Why think positively at all? Why not look at the situation rationally in the first phase of your thinking and then choose the most emotionally satisfying option in the second phase? This is surely superior to going around thinking positively about things … especially considering that you can deliberately add happiness to your day after you've made your 'relaxed wisdom' decision."

"I see your point, Mrs. Wombat. It is better to think rationally at the beginning of your decisions," said the possum.

"Yes. You can be as positive as you like about your final decision, but it doesn't make sense to be positive about decisions that would not be rational," agreed the wombat.

"Okay, let's look at another technique," said the possum.

"Very well. Another popular technique is 'Rational Skepticism'," said the wombat. "In this technique we basically ignore the emotional boss and go to our trusted adviser. We will be very skeptical in reviewing what our trusted adviser says. We require him to convince us of the truth of his assertions, we will not be satisfied with just any answers he may give."

* * *

"I'm not sure that it's worth the effort to try to get wealthier," said the emotional emu.

"Thanks for that but I'm not really interested in your opinion," said the possum. "I am going to talk to our trusted adviser."

The emu slumped down. He was used to being treated like this.

"Mr. Tortoise, what is your view on the effort needed to get wealthier?" the possum asked.

The tortoise looked through his file notes. "Mr. Possum," he said, "my notes say that the effort can be great and the results are not guaranteed."

"I see," said the possum. "What information is that based on?"

"Observations of creatures in real life show that it is not easy to become wealthy," replied the tortoise. "Also, many creatures fail and even the rich can lose their money when times change."

"I'm not satisfied with those observations," said the possum. "I was hoping for more substantial information than that. I think we had better explore the possibilities that are available in the world and form conclusions from that."

"Yes, Mr. Possum," said the tortoise obediently.

* * *

"Okay, and what's wrong with this technique, Mrs. Wombat?" asked the possum.

"Nothing, except that it doesn't really help your emotional boss and can be too demanding of your trusted adviser," said the wombat.

"And how much help should we give our emotional boss?" asked the possum. "Also, isn't it better to not trust our trusted adviser and check what he says?"

"Of course it's better to check what our trusted adviser is saying," said the wombat, "but it doesn't follow that we need to be harsh with him or demand perfection in everything he says. Sometimes just a little information and certainty is enough to make a valid decision.

"As for our emotional boss, it is not necessary to torment him and push him around – we can come to an amicable agreement where he is happy and we are still being wise in our decisions. That is what relaxed wisdom is all about."

"I see. That makes sense, Mrs. Wombat," said the possum. "Rational Skepticism is too harsh and does not make us happy."

"Yes. It can make us feel more confident about the decisions we have a lot of information about, but generally it does not make us happy and also we tend to worry too much about the quality of our decisions. We don't usually need to be so accurate about what we know. In many cases a little information is enough," explained the wombat.

"I agree, Mrs. Wombat, but how do you know when the information you have is enough to make a good decision?" asked the possum.

"The fundamental thing you have to realize is how much your trusted adviser actually knows. If you 'Know Yourself!' then you will know what information your trusted adviser is basing his decisions on. That way your evaluation of the accuracy of his answers will be reliable and you will know what you should do," said the wombat. "Apart from that, you should bear in mind what we discussed earlier about what evidence is acceptable in a court of law. We can trust direct experience for specific events and expert opinions for more complicated analysis."

"So we can trust our trusted adviser's views about specific events in our past, but not his assessment of complex areas which he doesn't know much about," said the possum.

"Precisely," agreed the wombat. "And often that will be enough. If it isn't, we can seek the advice of experts or learn more ourselves."

"Yes," agreed the possum.

"Moving on," said the wombat, "other techniques that the world proposes include 'Getting Rich' or 'Getting Powerful'.

"Right," said the possum.

"These don't work within your mind but outside it. The idea is that your circumstances change and so your emotional boss is much happier and less concerned," said the wombat.

* * *

"I'm glad I'm wealthier," said the emotional emu. "I feel much better about myself and my position in the world."

"Really?" said the possum. "That is interesting."

"Yes. I'm a very happy bird," said the emu.

"I can see that," said the possum. "I wonder what the tortoise would say." He went over to the trusted adviser. "What do you think about us being wealthier, Mr. Tortoise?" he asked.

The tortoise looked at his notes lazily. "It seems okay to me. We're well-off," he read.

"So it's a good thing then?" asked the possum.

"Of course. What do you think?" said the tortoise.

The emotional emu smiled over at them.

* * *

"It sounds good when you've got wealth," observed the possum.

"Sure, it can be," agreed the wombat, "except that you don't always have it, and even when you do it is never enough to do everything in life. Your emotional boss can still get upset and have a bad time no matter how wealthy you are."

"But on the whole he is less likely to get upset," said the possum.

"I'm not sure I can agree," replied the wombat. "I think a wealthy or powerful creature can still experience plenty of upsetting bad days."

"Really?" said the possum. "I suppose that's right."

"Yes, it is," said the wombat. "Relaxed wisdom would be better for dealing with those bad days."

"Hmm. I think you're right," agreed the possum.

"And don't forget the effort it could take to get rich. You may have to spend all your time working on it and never achieve it. Your whole life could become the pursuit of wealth or power and never feeling satisfied with what you have," warned the wombat.

"Indeed. Better to be wise about what you desire," agreed the possum. "If your emotional emu is ecstatically happy and you have enough money and power for practical needs then what use is it to you to pursue more!"

"That's right, Mr. Possum. That's exactly right."

* * *

"I'm happy with what we have," said the emotional emu.

"I'm glad to hear that," said the possum.

"Yes. We are well-off because we have enough to get by," said the emu. "It's foolish to run after more than you really need."

"Especially when you have enough to be really happy," agreed the possum.

"Yes," said the serious tortoise. "The things that really matter in life are family, friends, happy moments, saving creatures' lives, living your dreams, sunsets, staying true to your principles … and so on. If you do those things and also feel happy then you are rich and powerful enough."

The emu, the possum and the tortoise smiled at each other knowingly.

"The things that really matter in life are..."

* * *

"Are there any other techniques you would like to discuss, Mrs. Wombat?" asked the possum.

"Yes. I would like to look at the more 'spiritual' techniques recommended by the world," said the wombat. "If you believe in some sort of spiritual view then it can make sense for you to use its techniques."

* * *

"I feel upset, Mr. Possum," said the emotional emu.

"Then let's use a spiritual technique to make you feel better," suggested the possum.

"Meditation would be good," said the tortoise.

"Okay, let's meditate a little," agreed the emu.

As the possum meditated a feeling of calm enveloped them. The emu relaxed and sat down, the tortoise put his files away and just stared into space. The possum concentrated on his breathing – counting each breath in sets of ten. Soon he was thinking of nothing at all, just the counting of each breath. After ten minutes of this they all felt much better.

* * *

"I'm not sure you have to believe in all that much in order to meditate, Mrs. Wombat," said the possum.

"Possibly not, Mr. Possum," agreed the wombat. "But if you wanted to use some other 'spiritual' technique, such as praying to God, then you would have to believe in some religious view."

"I guess so," said the possum. "Say you do believe in a religious view or already practice meditation – what is wrong with this compared to relaxed wisdom?"

"Nothing," said the wombat, "except that none of these things is a substitute for wisdom. Wisdom must come first in your list of things to do."

"Why, Mrs. Wombat?"

"Because anything you believe or do should make sense, Mr. Possum," replied the wombat. "Even in spiritual matters it is possible to be reasonably sensible about what you believe."

"I see," said the possum. "I understand that but I'm not sure everyone would … and religion is such a difficult area to prove one way or the other."

"Possibly," agreed the wombat, "but I think that most creatures understand that you should be sensible about your beliefs. The problem is more to do with their lack of understanding of their emotional boss and their trusted adviser than with choosing what religion makes sense."

"So the issue is relaxed wisdom, not religion," said the possum.

"That's right," agreed the wombat.

* * *

"How did your discussion with Mrs. Wombat go today, honey?" the possum's wife asked later that night.

"Very well, thank you dear," replied the possum, kissing her on the cheek. "Today we talked about the other options proposed by the world, such as spiritual enlightenment or being wealthy."

"And which one was best?" asked his wife.

"We concluded that relaxed wisdom must come first, before you look at any other options," said the possum.

"I see," said the possum's wife. "And what might that mean for us?"

"I'm not sure honey, we'd have to discuss it," replied the possum, "but I suppose it would mean that we should use the relaxed wisdom techniques when making our decisions."

The possum's wife thought about this. "I'm not sure what that would mean, honey," she said. "I'd have to see what it was like."

"Of course," agreed the possum.

Things You Can Do

1. What do you think about Positive Thinking? Is this a technique you already use or would like to use? Do you think it opens up possibilities that we would otherwise avoid? How does being rational enough in our lives compare with that? What do you think about the wombat's statement that: "You can be as positive as you like about your final decisions, but it doesn't make sense to be positive about decisions that would not be rational."?

2. What do you feel about Rational Skepticism? Is this similar to how you make decisions now? Do you think it is always necessary to be this strict in your decision making?

3. Do you think wealth or power can solve your problems in life? How much wealth or power will you need? How do you plan to get this?

4. Do you believe in some sort of spiritual view? Do you think you should be sensible about what you believe, or do you think there are other ways to know the truth? Where would you put "relaxed wisdom" in relation to your own beliefs?

Farewell

"I'd like to thank you for all the help you've given me, Mrs. Wombat," said the possum. "I feel that it is really changing my life and, more importantly, it is changing me as well."

"I'm glad to hear it," said the wombat. "It's been a pleasure to help you. Let's review what we have discussed and see how it applies to your original problem."

The possum nodded.

"We talked about the basic meaning of relaxed wisdom, which is to see yourself as being like three creatures: your true self, an emotional boss 'emu', and a serious trusted adviser 'tortoise'. The emu represents your emotions, which it's okay to satisfy, but only after you have applied your wisdom first. The tortoise represents the ideas which have come from your experiences and need to be checked to see if they are really wise."

"Yes," said the possum.

"Relaxed wisdom aims to give you the maximum happiness possible while still remaining wise about what you do. We discussed seven techniques for achieving this:

1 Ask an Expert!

2 Go Inside!

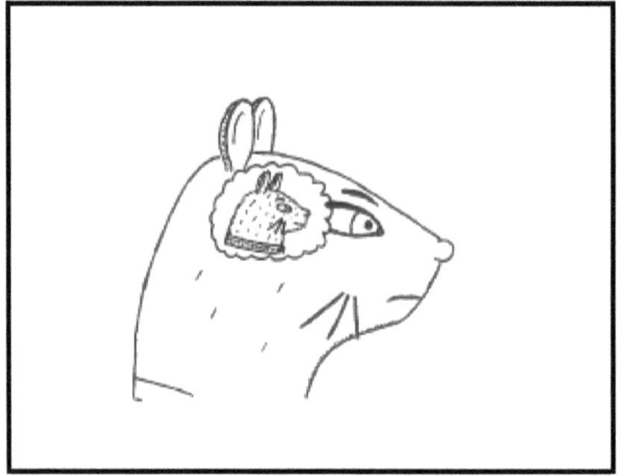

3 Get Away!

4 Get Familiar!

5 Know Yourself!

6 Think Again!

7 Make Perfect Decisions and Add Happiness!

"Wonderful techniques," commented the possum.

"Thank you. Yes they are," said the wombat. "How does all this relate to your original problem with your life? Well, by asking experts, going inside the nature of the other creatures and the situation, getting away both in reality and in your mind, getting familiar with your feelings, knowing yourself and how you think, thinking again, and making perfect decisions and adding happiness you have realized a lot about what was going on and what is really important to you in life.

"You have realized that it is not necessary to be extremely wealthy and powerful in order to be happy: you only need enough wealth and power for practical purposes and to get through your life. That leaves you free to concentrate on happiness … on adding happy thoughts and experiences to your day," said the wombat.

"That is interesting, Mrs. Wombat," said the possum. "So my family does not need vast amounts of wealth and power in order to be happy. That is not to say that we don't need more than we have now, and it is not wrong to enjoy the benefits of wealth and power if you have them, but what we really need to consider is how much effort we're willing to make versus how much happiness we can expect wealth and power to give us."

"That's right, Mr. Possum," agreed the wombat. "Now in regard to your problems with your wife and children and the thoughts in your own mind you have learnt to 'Go Inside!' the mind of the other creatures and to 'Get Familiar!' with your own feelings and 'Know Yourself!' and why you think what you do. With these and other techniques you can gain an insight into what the other creatures are thinking and feeling and adjust your behavior to match. You can achieve better results with others through your understanding of their minds. Also, as you come to understand yourself better you will learn which problems are real and which are just caused by your own view of life."

"Yes, that certainly happened to me," said the possum.

"Good," said the wombat. "Then I think we are finished. Go out into the world and practice these relaxed wisdom techniques and be happier and wiser in your life."

"Yes, I will," said the possum. "Thank you so much for helping me, Mrs. Wombat."

"It was my pleasure, Mr. Possum," smiled the wombat.

* * *

That night the possum called his family together for a discussion.

"I have learnt a lot from Mrs. Wombat," he told them, "and I have come to realize that I was not acting wisely and happily in my life. I hope to improve myself over time by practicing the relaxed wisdom techniques Mrs. Wombat taught me.

"One thing was very clear: it is not necessary to be very wealthy to be happy, and you don't need to be very powerful, all you need is enough for practical purposes. That doesn't mean that you can't enjoy the wealth and power you have, you just have to bear in mind that it takes effort to get more and it may not be worth it to you in terms of happiness."

"Yes, that makes sense," agreed the possum's wife. "You have to work out how much effort you're willing to make for how much happiness."

The children watched their parents with interest.

"Yes, and there are other ways to be happy than buying things or having the power to tell other creatures what to do," said the possum.

"Yes," said his wife.

The possum kissed her cheek and she hugged him back.

"So I don't mind taking a job in the town or moving to a more productive area," said the possum, "if that would make everyone happier. As long as we can spend time together that would be all right."

"That's very kind of you, honey," said the possum's wife. "I'm not sure we need all that much based on what you have said about happiness, but perhaps a little more would be nice."

"Okay," said the possum. "Does everyone agree?"

The children nodded thoughtfully.

"Good. Then let's proceed with our happier and wiser life together," said the possum.

They all smiled at each other.

"Let's proceed with our happier and wiser life together."

About the Author

Geoff Pridham has been seeking the answers to leading the best possible life ever since he first asked the question in 1976: "Why do we believe the things that we do?" Since then he has made it his mission to find out what really matters and how we can live happier and wiser lives. He has left no stone unturned in his quest for this knowledge – studying philosophy, psychology, biology, religion, art, history, science, lateral thinking and any other field that could help us find the truth about life.

After more than 30 years of work Geoff says: "We have a lot to learn about our true place in the universe, but with a practical and realistic approach we really can lead happier and wiser lives. It's not about academic theories but the things that real life teaches us. Anyone who is sincere can take the journey to a better life."

Geoff works as an IT professional and lives happily in Sydney, Australia with his lovely wife.

www.ingramcontent.com/pod-product-compliance
Ingram Content Group UK Ltd.
Pitfield, Milton Keynes, MK11 3LW, UK
UKHW041942190726
13854UKWH00004B/1745